REAGAN INSIDE OUT

Reagan poses manfully as a youngster in Illinois.

REAGAN INSIDE OUT

Bob Slosser

WORD BOOKS
PUBLISHER
WACO, TEXAS

A DIVISION OF
WORD, INCORPORATED

Grateful acknowledgment is made for permission to use material from the following:
    Reagan by Lou Cannon. Reprinted by permission of G. P. Putnam's Sons, New York. Copyright © 1982 by Lou Cannon.
    The Real Reagan by Frank van der Linden. Reprinted by permission of William Morrow & Co., Inc., New York. Copyright © 1981 by Frank van der Linden.
    The Reagans: A Personal Portrait by Peter Hannaford. Reprinted by permission of Coward-McCann, Inc., New York. Copyright © 1982 by Peter D. Hannaford.
    Sincerely, Ronald Reagan, edited by Helene von Damm, Berkley Books, New York. Copyright © 1981.

Library of Congress Cataloging in Publication Data
Slosser, Bob.
   Reagan inside out.
   Bibliography: p.
   1. Reagan, Ronald—Religion.   2. Presidents—United States—Biography.   I. Title.
#877.2.S58   1984   973.927'092'4   84–2193
ISBN 0–08499—0376–9

Printed in the United States of America

For *McCandlish Phillips*

A reporter worthy of the name

Contents

Preface

Ronald Reagan is on his way to becoming one of our country's most controversial presidents. Emotions over him run high, for and against. He presides over one of the most explosive periods in our nation's life. Emotions over it run high, too.

Watching the nation's struggles and Reagan's efforts to provide leadership, I kept hearing variations of one question: How does the man think? Or, what causes him to think the way he does? People with religious underpinnings to their views framed their queries in language like this: Is he really a believer?

Deciding to dig into the matter, I ran into a second question that must inevitably follow if one is to give national significance to the first: Can a man holding Reagan's beliefs govern a nation like the United States and bring forth meaningful change?

As a result, this book at times proceeds along two tracks, although they eventually merge, true to the thesis that, despite man's tendency to compartmentalize his life, the spiritual and the physical worlds are in reality inextricable.

One might say I have attempted to paint a spiritual portrait of our fortieth president, set in the secular context of politics and world events.

I've had help from every part of the country, and I'm grateful for it, but I am not at liberty to name every name, so I will name none but my indefatigable secretary, scheduler, and counselor, Anita Leftwich, who bore the brunt of a tight deadline.

BOB SLOSSER
Virginia Beach, Virginia
October, 1983

9

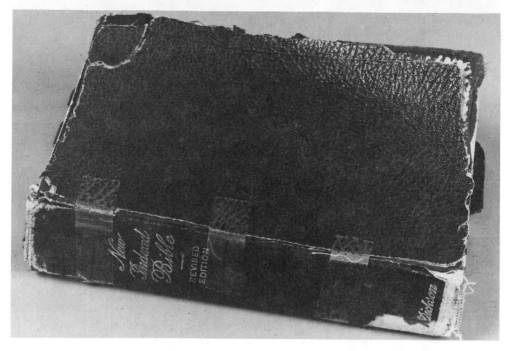

Here is the well-used Bible of President Reagan's mother, Nelle, from which he was trained in his early years.

Among the many well-marked passages in Nelle Reagan's Bible is 2 Chronicles 7:14. In the margin she wrote, "A most wonderful verse for the healing of the nations." (Official Photographs—The White House)

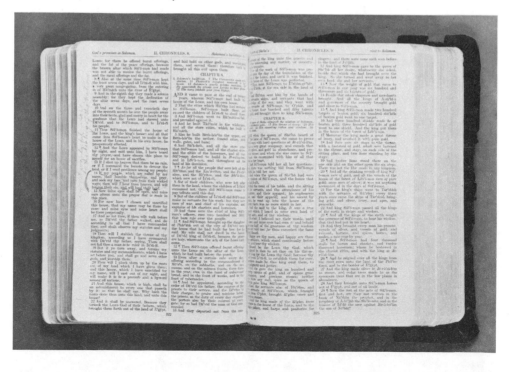

REAGAN INSIDE OUT

The Reagan family in Illinois: Jack and Neil, Ronald and Nelle.
(Official Photograph—The White House)

★ ★ ★ ★ ★ ★ ★ ★ ★ ★ ★ ★ ★ *1* ★ ★ ★ ★ ★ ★ ★ ★ ★ ★ ★ ★ ★

A Prophecy

THE AFTERNOON SUNLIGHT was dimming, thrusting the spacious living room into browns and golds. It was that magic moment peculiar to the fall of the year, whether in California or Maine, when it is neither day nor dusk. Childhood memories are often filled with Sunday afternoons like that, memories of a special day.

Seven sharply different people drifted into that moment on this Sunday afternoon in October, 1970, stepping almost aimlessly toward the foyer of a stately Tudor home in Sacramento. They were talking rather softly, but running over one another's words as they edged toward the entrance.

One moved in front, then hesitated, looking back at the rest. That was Herbert E. Ellingwood. He was, in a fashion, herding four of the others, who were obviously visitors. He was just a whisper out of rhythm with them—not awkward, perhaps tentative. They were getting ready to say good-bye and that heightened everyone's uncertainty.

Ronald Reagan was smiling and nodding as he turned his head toward Pat Boone, whose smile caused his entire face to glisten. Nancy Reagan watched the two of them momentarily, the barest trace of a smile on her lips, and then she whispered two or three words to Shirley Boone. Two rather short men, Harald Bredesen and George Otis, moved toward Ronald Reagan and Boone. Both were silent, and Bredesen seemed to be studying the floor.

Suddenly, everyone stopped. In the split-second of stillness, they looked at one another. Then one of the men—Boone or Bredesen—said, "Governor, would you mind if we prayed a moment with you and Mrs. Reagan?"

13

"We'd appreciate that." Reagan's face remained bright and pleasant, but eased ever so slightly toward seriousness.

It was hard to tell who moved first, probably Boone, but in a sort of chain reaction, the seven took hold of each other's hands and made an uneven circle. For an instant, they were like little children, each looking first to the right and down at one set of hands and then left to the other. Only Boone seemed thoroughly at ease, but long friendship had broken all barriers between him and all those there, including the Reagans, their hosts. He had a happy smile on his face. Otis and Bredesen were obviously tense. Nancy's expression was quizzical, but relaxed.

All seven closed their eyes. Reagan bowed his head sharply; Nancy's remained fairly level. The others tilted theirs a bit.

Otis, standing to Reagan's left, remembered the few seconds of awkward silence that followed. "It was a little tense," he said, "a bit embarrassing. We didn't know how they felt about doing that, you know. Suddenly we realized we might be a little presumptuous."

And that's the way they stood, holding hands, eyes closed. Otis thought the seconds seemed like minutes. He cleared his throat, and began to pray, "Lord, we thank you for the chance to be here together. . . ." It was very general, the kind of prayer offered at large and small gatherings all across the land. It was so ordinary that no one remembered much of it.

"I was just sort of praying from the head," Otis said. "I was saying those things you'd expect—you know, thanking the Lord for the Reagans, their hospitality, and that sort of thing."

That went on for ten or fifteen seconds, and then it changed. "Everything shifted from my head to the spirit—*the* Spirit," Otis recalled. "The Holy Spirit came upon me and I knew it. In fact, I was embarrassed. There was this pulsing in my arm. And my hand—the one holding Governor Reagan's hand—was shaking. I didn't know what to do. I just didn't want this thing to be happening. I can remember that even as I was speaking, I was working, you know, tensing my muscles and concentrating, and doing everything I could to stop that shaking.

"It wasn't a wild swinging or anything like that. But it was a definite, pulsing shaking. And I made a great physical effort to stop it—but I couldn't."

As this was going on, the content of Otis' prayer changed completely. His voice remained essentially the same, although the words came much more steadily and intently. They spoke specifically to Ronald

Reagan and referred to him as "My son." They recognized his role as leader of the state that was indeed the size of many nations. His "labor" was described as "pleasing."

The foyer was absolutely still and silent. The only sound was George's voice. Everyone's eyes were closed.

"If you walk uprightly before Me, you will reside at 1600 Pennsylvania Avenue."

The words ended. The silence held for three or four seconds. Eyes began to open, and the seven rather sheepishly let go of hands.

Reagan took a deep breath and turned and looked into Otis' face. All he said was a very audible "Well!" It was almost as though he were exhaling.

Otis was struck by the calm expression on Reagan's face. "I was really concerned about how he might have taken it all," George remembered. "But the expression on his face was kind, wholesome—a receptive look, you know. It was not gushy or sentimental or any of that. He just said, 'Well,' and that was that. We all said good-bye, and we left."

Ellingwood, the Governor's legal affairs secretary, had driven the Boones, Bredesen, and Otis from the airport several hours before the big Christian rally that had brought them all from Southern California. Pat and Ron had been friends for some time, so a visit seemed natural, although Reagan was deep into the pressure of his campaign for reelection as Governor of California. Pat had been especially eager to talk about his own recent experiences as a serious-minded Christian and had asked his two close friends along with him.

"I had known that Reagan was under tremendous pressure from the campaign," Bredesen said later, "and I had anticipated seeing a pressured, harried-looking person. But when he opened the door he just stood there, sort of leaning up against the door in the most casual, boyish, carefree way. I was absolutely amazed."

Before taking the guests inside, the governor showed them around the grounds, the swimming pool, and the patio. It was a dazzling, sunny October day, and Reagan, wearing gray slacks and a long-sleeved open-necked sport shirt, seemed to enjoy it fully.

Bredesen recounted: "I remember that later on I remarked about how well and how relaxed he seemed despite the pressures that obviously were on him, and he said, 'Well, I determined very early in my political career that I would never make decisions on the basis of votes gained or lost, but whether it was right or wrong.' He paused, and said with a wide grin, 'This has relieved me of a great deal of tension.' "

After the tour, they went inside the big home, which Reagan leased from a group of wealthy friends who bought it after Ron and Nancy had determined the old Governor's Mansion was not the place to bring up young Ron and Patti.

They sat in the long, simple and tasteful living room, and Reagan quickly went into an alcove and returned with soft drinks for everyone. "There was not a question as to anything stronger," Otis recalled. "He simply brought soft drinks."

Much of the conversation dealt with spiritual matters. Reagan asked questions, and offered his opinions. But he listened a lot. Otis remembered the discussions as "quietly intense."

At one point, Reagan spoke of a recent visit by Billy Graham. He said he had been sick in bed and the evangelist had dropped in. Those present that afternoon reconstructed the account as follows:

"Billy shared with me a very interesting conversation he had had with Chancellor Adenauer [of West Germany]," Reagan said. "It seems that the chancellor asked him: 'Billy, do you know what the next great event of world history is going to be?' And Billy replied, 'I wish you'd tell me.'

" 'The return of Jesus Christ,' Adenauer said.

"And the chancellor went on, 'As you know, Billy, I'm a student of the Scriptures, especially of prophetic eschatology, and I have discovered in my studies that, though there are many of these prophecies that must be fulfilled before Christ returns, many have long since been fulfilled. Today all prophetic eschatology focuses on this present period of world history as the one in which He will come back.' "

. With that, Bredesen recalled, Reagan began to discuss the biblical prophecies that had been fulfilled, mostly those pertaining to the Jews and the birth of the State of Israel in 1948. He especially noted the words of Jesus in Luke's Gospel that many conservative scholars believe point to the Six-Day War in 1967 and Israel's re-establishment of Jewish control of Jerusalem for the first time since Nebuchadnezzar of Babylon destroyed the city in 587 B.C.: Jerusalem will be trodden down by the Gentiles, until the times of the Gentiles are fulfilled.[1]

When Reagan concluded, Bredesen jumped in: "Governor, you've left off the most important area of fulfilled prophecy of all."

"What's that?" he asked.

"Just before Jesus Christ comes back, there will be a tremendous outpouring of the Holy Spirit on a scale not seen since the Day of Pentecost." Bredesen paused, smiling brightly, and Reagan pursed his lips, looking into Harald's face.

"James tells us: 'Be patient therefore, brethren, unto the coming of the Lord, for as the husbandman sowed his seed and waiteth for the precious fruits of the earth, and hath long patience for it, until he has received the early and the latter rain, be ye also patient; establish your hearts: for the coming of the Lord draweth nigh.' "[2]

Reagan merely nodded his head. Harald pressed on. "Well, as you probably know, there are two rainy seasons in Israel—the early rain, which prepares the soil for the reception of the seed and germinates the seed after it has been sown and nurses it along while it sends down its roots. Then will come a period of relative drought, in which the grain seems to be making very little headway. And then comes the final rain—the latter rain—which brings the grain to a head overnight, for the return of the husbandman."

Again, the governor nodded his head. "What will this latter rain be?" he asked.

A boyish smile burst onto Bredesen's face. "Well, there's a classic commentary for evangelicals for more than a hundred years—Jamieson, Fausset, and Brown, British scholars—and they say this will probably be 'another Pentecost-like effusion,' preparing the church—the harvest, for the return of the husbandman."

Everyone in the room was listening to Reagan and Bredesen by this time. The sun's rays splashed across the floor, brightening the intensity of the discussion. Boone looked first at the governor and then back at Harald.

"Governor," Harald spoke softly, leaning forward in his chair, "I'm sure you agree that it's unusual to get an archconservative and an archliberal and the Scriptures all to agree." He smiled quickly. "It would be more than a coincidence if they agreed, wouldn't you say?"

Reagan was still, then grinned. "That I would."

"Well," Harald said, "I'd like to give you a quotation from the president of Moody Bible Institute—the conservative—and one from a professor at Harvard Theological Seminary—the liberal. Maybe you can tell me which is which."

Harald paused just for a second, touched his fingertips together, then began: "Commenting on the sixteenth chapter of Mark, the Great Commission, this theologian says, 'Healing the sick, casting out demons, speaking in new tongues, still occurs in the foreign mission field and will doubtless become well-nigh universal just before the return of Christ.' "

Bredesen hesitated for a moment and asked Reagan, "Was that Harvard or was it Moody?"

Reagan laughed. "Before I tell you, I'd like to hear quotation number two."

"Okay," Harald said. "I don't blame you. Here's number two: 'In prophetic eschatology, the consummation of the kingdom and the ushering in of the eternal reign of Christ will be preceded by a vast resurgence of charismatic happenings, and in that day, both leaders and people will be Spirit-filled and Spirit-empowered on a scale hitherto unknown.' "

Harald stopped. His eyes were wide, and he smiled. But Reagan didn't give him a chance to say anything further. "On the basis of vocabulary alone, I know that the latter had to be Harvard," he chuckled. "You'll always know a Harvard theologian; he'll never be guilty of using a short word where a long one will do."

"That's right," Harald said. "But note that both men—archconservative and archliberal—are saying just what the Scriptures say. Just before Jesus Christ comes back, there will be 'a vast resurgence of charismatic happenings. And in that day, both leaders and people will be Spirit-filled and Spirit-empowered on a scale hitherto unknown.' "

He paused for just a second. "And, governor, that day is upon us. And that's why we're here. That's what we—or at least part of what we wanted to share with you."

Small talk followed, and the visitors soon rose to leave—Pat Boone, singer, entertainer, celebrity, outspoken Christian; his wife; Harald Bredesen, former pastor, television interviewer, and minister to world leaders; George Otis of High Adventure Ministries, later founder of TV and radio stations in the Middle East.

It was a strange assortment of people. It had been a rather strange afternoon.

Questioned later, Otis was particularly struck by the fact that his prayer-turned-prophecy had been so precise about Reagan's future. "God had a plan," he said, "but it was conditional. It hinged on Reagan's actions."

Most emphatically, he was dismayed about the shaking of his hand during the prayer, concerned that Reagan might have thought him eccentric. But his amazement was increased when he later learned from Ellingwood, who had been on the right side of Reagan, that the governor's other hand had been shaking similarly to Otis's. Elling-wood himself recalled years later that he somehow felt a "bolt of electricity" as he clasped Reagan's hand.

"I can only think that the prophecy was being authenticated to the governor," Otis said.

Pressed as to his opinion of Governor Reagan that day, he said: "Well, as you may know, I've always liked the man. I thought he was great. But, remember, there wasn't a lot of talk about his being president at that time. I sure hadn't talked about it—certainly not up to the time of that word there in his house."

Bredesen, some time later, recalled that he had been much impressed by Reagan's relaxed, boyish appearance and by his friendliness. And he had found the governor's knowledge of the Bible to be deeper than he expected. Remembering Nancy, he said, "I think she may have been a little threatened by us but she certainly was kind and friendly. I'm not sure how comfortable she was though."

As for presidential qualities, that afternoon he preferred to wait and see.

The President

IT WAS TEN YEARS later. Ronald Reagan had been elected President of the United States by a large margin. Pat Boone, in Washington on business a few days after the election, found himself thinking of his old friend as midnight approached.

Since it was only nine o'clock in California, he telephoned across the country to the Reagans' Pacific Palisades home.

"Nancy answered," he remembered, "and she said, 'We're in bed, but the TV is on. We just felt like we should get to bed early tonight.' "

After a few moments of light-hearted talk, she put Reagan on the phone.

"Hello, Mr. President!" Boone almost sang the words. "Boy, how great that sounds!"

"It sounds pretty good to me, too," the president-elect chuckled.

After congratulating him—"he was feeling great about it all"— Boone asked if he remembered the prayer in Sacramento, "the time we joined hands and prayed, and we had a sense you were being called to something higher."

Without hesitation, according to Boone, Reagan replied enthusiastically, "Of course I do."

"We didn't get into any in-depth conversation about it," Boone recalled, "but I said something like 'It appears we were right-on, and we know you're going to make a great president.' "

To have lost sight of that prophetic word would have been understandable. Its fulfillment certainly did not come overnight. Following a half-hearted effort against Richard Nixon for the GOP nomination in 1968, the Californian sat quietly by in 1972 and then went all out in 1976 to try unsuccessfully to deny the nomination to Gerald Ford, to the dismay of the Republican establishment.

After that, many of the experts wrote Reagan off as too old. He would, after all, turn seventy just two weeks after taking office should he achieve the impossible in 1980.

George Otis more and more resembled a false prophet.

Nonetheless, on the evening of 13 November 1979, Ronald Reagan appeared at the New York Hilton in territory far from his nurturing West to declare, "I am here tonight to announce my intention to seek the Republican nomination for President of the United States."

His intention was not founded on the prophecy; neither did he reject it. Rather, his decision was based on a conviction hammered out over a decade and a half that he understood the United States and its needs and that he could lead the people to fulfillment. In his view, conditions had deteriorated badly since another man of good will, Jimmy Carter, had felt a similar conviction and had risen to the presidency. Something must be done.

Announcing his candidacy, he declared, "I am totally unwilling to see this country fail in its obligation to itself and to the other free peoples of the world."

Actually, Reagan had been running intently toward 1980 for the previous year and a half. That night in New York, his delivery, if not all the content, had been shaped to its husky best. Many politicians and newsmen were unimpressed by what they heard but, as was so often the case with this actor-turned-politician, the millions watching on television were stimulated. The cameras picked up no trace of the staff dissension that was straining this man so dependent on unity. They could not see the campaign mismanagement, the tendency to hide the real Reagan, that would soon bring reorganization. They heard a man who sounded like them.

"The crisis we face is not the result of any failure of the American spirit," he said firmly, without harshness. "It is a failure of our leaders to establish rational goals and give our people something to order their lives by. If I am elected, I shall regard my election as proof that the people of the United States have decided to set a new agenda and have recognized that the human spirit thrives best when goals are set and progress can be measured in their achievement."

Pounding at inflation and weakness in the American economy, massive government growth, and declining stature internationally, he predicted that the people wanted "a leader who will unleash their great strength and remove the roadblocks government has put in their way."

Then, with the wide-eyed, little-boy look that often surfaces in moments of seriousness, he said simply: "I want to do that more than anything I've ever wanted. And it's something that I believe with God's help I *can* do."

The professionals saw those last two sentences as a cliché. But were they? Reagan watchers had come to believe that those remarks, perhaps corny, revealed the true man. He *did* want to heal what he believed to be the sickness in his beloved land. He was not embarrassed by calling it his beloved land. He was serious when he invoked God's help.

That was the man Reagan, the last of ten Republicans to declare their candidacy for 1980, the one who rolled on to win the party's nomination with ease after some tentative early moments, arising primarily from his organizational and strategy problems. Threaded through those months of campaigning were some unusual, inner-man ideas and phrases that continued to be lost on the politicians and the newsmen but were noted by millions of disenchanted voters.

"I believe this nation hungers for a spiritual revival," he said frequently, insisting that "we have a rendezvous with destiny."

He spoke often of America's becoming "a city on a hill," quoting John Winthrop's admonition to the Pilgrims: "The eyes of all people are upon us so that if we shall deal falsely with our God in this work we have undertaken and so cause Him to withdraw His present help from us, we shall be made a story and a byword throughout the world."

Perhaps one of the most powerful such moments came on the night he accepted the party nomination at the national convention in Detroit's Joe Louis Arena. It was not a graceful moment, but a certain awkwardness in execution often seems to blend into a special Reagan graciousness that translates into persuasiveness. Looking up, and then down, and then back up, he seemed small and even insecure behind the massive convention podium.

Then he blurted, "I'll confess that I've been a little afraid to suggest what I'm going to suggest." He paused slightly. "I'm more afraid not to—that we begin our crusade joined together in a moment of silent prayer."

He allowed ten seconds or more to pass, although it seemed longer, and he looked up. Everyone was on his side in that moment. "God bless America," he said huskily.

Moments like that are difficult to assess. Newsmen generally have no frame of reference from which to make a judgment. They figure the words are throwaway lines, superficial at best. Those who do not themselves engage in prayer find it difficult to imagine that anyone takes it seriously. They're not evil in their assessments, but merely lacking the experience to judge the impact of such actions—either with voters or with God.

And newsmen are not alone. Others in the so-called political nation, which will be discussed in some detail later, have the same weakness. These include politicians, academicians, big business executives, labor leaders, television and film figures, authors, and other opinion makers.

As a result, the "system" was blind-sided by the runaway victory in the 1980 race for the presidency, fooled by the Reagan mystery. The unhappiness with Carter was recognized, but the closing rush to the westerner assumed proportions in the countryside that were not foreseen.

In his biography of this actor, screen union leader, corporate spokesman, and two-term governor, newsman Lou Cannon saw past the politics to at least part of the quality of Reagan's appeal when he wrote some time later: "Reagan profited from Watergate because it encouraged voters to look at the human dimension of their leaders, a yardstick by which Reagan is better measured than by, say, an examination of his intimate knowledge of the merits of competing strategic weapons systems."[1]

He added: "Campaigns are won in the hearts of men before they are won at the ballot box. They are won by candidates doing what they do best and knowing themselves and feeling secure about what they are saying."[2]

Reagan had talked to the people.

The Californian was taking a shower when he learned he had been elected. It was about 5:30 in the afternoon, West Coast time. For the rest of the night, his best line was "I just can't believe it." He repeated it dozens of times, first at a dinner with close friends in Bel Air, then at a reception on the top floor of the Century Plaza, and finally at a jubilant party of supporters in the hotel's ballroom.

But the former governor *could* believe it. He had not been confident of the electoral landslide that broke loose, but he had worked to win. He had *expected* to win.

This showed clearly in his extemporaneous remarks to the happy throng in the ballroom. "I'm not frightened by what lies ahead and

I don't believe the American people are frightened," he said, certain of his interpretation of the mood of America. "Together, we are going to do what has to be done. We're going to put America back to work again."

He knew his audience, and once again, he let his inner man show:

"When I accepted your nomination for president, I hesitatingly asked for your prayers at that moment. I won't ask for them at this particular moment, but I will just say that I will be very happy to have them in the days ahead."

Ronald Reagan, the man from the West, was the first president in history to face west from the Capitol instead of east for his inauguration. He chose to gaze upon the marvelous monuments and memorials honoring the great leadership of America's past. An old-fashioned man, he was genuinely moved by recollections of "the giants on whose shoulders we stand."

And he continued a spiritual man that sunny January 20. "Let us renew our determination, our courage, and our strength," he said. "And let us renew our faith and hope. We have every right to dream heroic dreams."

There was the thread again, revealed in variations. Faith and hope. He apparently believed he knew how to put meat on those spiritual bones. He believed the people wanted him to make the effort.

It meant change. Sharp change. It called for hard, radical decisions in the White House, in the Congress, in the state houses and the town halls. But he apparently had faith and hope that the courage was there to make the decisions, even though it had not always been forthcoming in his eight years as Governor of California. But the forum was larger now. The pulpit was bigger. And the people were staring up at it, eager, expectant. As one sympathetic journalist wrote of the man who had just climbed into that pulpit: "Americans who look for a Big Daddy in the White House will not find one there. They will see, instead, a simple, earnest, courageous man who is seeking guidance from God."[3]

Peter Hannaford is a Reagan man. He worked hard to get him elected president. Reagan was, after all, the major client of his California-based public relations firm. As a wordsman, Hannaford fell upon one of those rare passages that, despite its generalities, captured in half a dozen sentences the essence of the incoming president and set the stage fairly and clearly for his administration:

> In Ronald Reagan's case, over a period of years he worked out a clear set of principles about the role of government and, on holding public office, *never altered his principles, though he was quite willing to compromise in terms of accomplishing specific program elements* [italics added]. As Governor of California, he proved he was consistent, but also practical. He knew that a successful chief executive and politician could not fight every battle as if it were Armageddon. His political acumen was and is probably based on many factors in his background: his mother's steadfast belief in God and good works in the temporal world; his father's good humor; his tolerance for idiosyncrasies and unconventionality, probably developed during his film career when he had to get along with a wide variety of temperaments; his instinct for negotiating, forged during his six terms as president of the Screen Actors' Guild; his belief that government was growing out of control, developed strongly in his years with General Electric and his many contacts with business people and plant workers.
>
> There was no reason to believe he would not apply the same approach to the federal government. Would he be served well by those around him, or would he suffer from the inevitable "turf" disputes that plague the early months of most administrations?[4]

Reagan was in the White House. The country loved him. His party held a majority in the Senate for the first time in twenty-six years. Republicans had gained in the House and given that body a more conservative flavor. He said he was on God's side. God seemed to be on his.

What now? Could he govern? Could anyone of his persuasion govern? Those were mysteries.

Enjoying a crescendo of popularity and enthusiasm that often accompanies a change in Washington administrations, the new president moved quickly and steadfastly on two broad fronts, much as his campaign and inauguration had forecast—economy and defense. He felt he must curb runaway inflation and spending, getting "the government off the backs" of the people, including business, and re-establish the United States as a credible leader of the Western world.

Edwin Meese III, counselor to the president, spoke of those goals three years later. "When the president came in," he said, "we had a 180-day plan—and basically a plan for the whole first year. We then extended that by what ought to happen in the second year. He set the objectives. One was to revitalize the economy, and the second was to rebuild our national defenses."

Reflecting on the need for "leading" and not always merely "reacting" to situations, which is a temptation with any large organization, whether a corporation or a government, Meese went on: "In a sense you could say we were reacting to a situation—one that had been building up for a long time—but we were taking the lead on what we ought to be doing, rather than waiting for Congress to pass bills and we then decide what to do about them. So that was where the president dominated the agenda.

"Then in the second half of the second year, we had a major midterm planning exercise throughout the whole government. . . . We met with every department head and every major agency head and developed what things we should be doing in the second two years. Each Cabinet council did the same thing. And so that set the agenda for the next year. So in that sense, we were again trying to get ahead of things rather than merely reacting."

These objectives, which would be expanded into regulatory areas, crime, education, and the like, obviously called for a major turnaround in the direction of the country in recent decades. Unusual steps would be required. But would the system, the establishment, the opinion leaders permit those steps?

Reagan's well-developed skills as a communicator were, as always, his most valuable asset as he attempted to establish himself and his team in the skeptical, cynical city of Washington. Even those who assumed they disagreed with everything he stood for found they couldn't help liking him. His charm—his earnestness, his sincerity—overpowered their natural hostility. A few minutes of conversation with him proved capable of modifying even the most hardened position.

Furthermore, Reagan was riding high with the people out across the land. He appeared to have a mandate, certainly in terms of the electoral process, and he knew how to reach out and touch those who had risen to his cause and propelled him into office when everyone thought his day had passed. He was magnificent on television and radio.

His toughest struggle, as is the case with so many newcomers to Washington, was with the press corps. Personal relationships were good, but his performance before them as a group left much to be desired. He seemed uncomfortable at news conferences—nervous or unprepared or both. He sometimes bobbled questions, and even gave wrong answers, which though later corrected still proved damaging.

A complicating factor for the president was his difficulty in hearing, tracing back to damage done in his acting days when a gun was fired close to his ear. Confusion caused by this weakness reached a point where an amplifier had to be installed in the presidential podium. (In 1983 he went a step further and began to wear a tiny hearing aid.)

But the problem was greater than this. Reagan simply had not mastered his subject matter well enough, probably because of inexperience in the job, to allow his communicative skills to take hold. And the anxiety caused by this showed. One of Washington's temperate and seasoned columnists, David Broder, worried about this weakness: "The comments on Capitol Hill and in embassies suggest that the tension and anxiety the president displays when answering questions about his policies are beginning to cause concern among those here and abroad who look to the White House for leadership."[5]

The White House staff worried more than Broder, scheduling fewer press conferences and working with the president to stretch out his answers and thus deal with fewer questions. In a word, Reagan became unnatural. "The relaxed sense of command and self-control that he communicated so advantageously in his 1980 campaign debates and in almost every formal speech he has made as president turns into a very tentative and tense performance in the press conferences," observed Broder.

Before long came a distinct sag. True, a number of Reagan's new directions for the government and the country, usually in modified form, slipped into place, almost imperceptibly at times. Inflation eased. But unemployment soared. Interest rates were unbelievably high. Recession—hard times—gripped many industrial regions. The ogre of budget deficits grew uglier and bigger.

Controversy raged over the size of defense and social entitlement expenditures, and a third monster grew in impact—interest paid on a worsening national debt. It seemed obvious that nothing approaching budget balance could be expected with these three items alone soaring into the hundreds of billions of dollars.

And so the struggle went.

Congress became tougher, especially after Democratic gains in the midterm elections, and the public outcry against recession became louder. With this, the complexion of Reagan's popularity changed. Uncertainty about his policy leadership was reflected in opinion polls, yet his personal standing held fairly high. Somehow, even though they railed against recession, the people were touched by his commitment to the changes he believed were necessary for restoration.

They remembered accounts of his words to the Cabinet as he sought additional reductions in domestic social spending in the face of recession and pressure for slashes in defense. Pressing for courageous action to correct the country's problems, he asked his officers: "Can anyone here say that if we can't do it, someone down the road can do it? And if no one does it, what happens to the country? All of us here know the economy would face an eventual collapse. I know it's a tremendous challenge, but ask yourselves: If not us, who? If not now, when?"

Such reports of his sincerity registered well with the population, even the portion that didn't see eye to eye with him. If he said in private what he was saying in public, then he must really mean it.

And he apparently did mean it, even when some of those closest to him were having second thoughts. There was the time late in his first year when the pressure was mounting to reverse his field and accept some increases in taxes, which he ultimately did even though he said he believed they were contrary to the best long-run interests of the country.

Again, Cannon captured the determination of the man:

> Even those who had known Reagan a long time would be touched by the faith he showed in his policies when there didn't seem to be much hope for them. Deaver [his closest aide] would remember the time on December 4, 1981, when Stockman [director of OMB] and Baker [chief of staff] had tried to win Reagan's support for "revenue enhancements." Reagan stubbornly shook his head. "Revenue enhancements," he said, "are by any other name a tax increase." Stockman and Baker left. Deaver lingered behind in the gathering gloom of the Oval Office, talking with the president he both protected and admired about the administration's dwindling economic options. Reagan reviewed what had been said to him, then shook his head. "You know, Mike," he said, "I just don't think that some of my people believe in my program the way I do."[6]

Such episodes graphically bore out his typical one-liner aimed at critics who argued that he was too simplistic in his approach to complex difficulties: There *are* simple answers to the nation's problems, but not *easy* ones.

As the weeks and months evolved into years, Reagan passed the midway point in his term and the darkness of recession seemed to be paling. Unemployment was still painfully high, but other indicators showed brightness. The inflation rate remained low. Business was getting stronger. The temper of the people generally seemed better. A quiet confidence appeared to be replacing jitters.

Why? Was improvement inevitable? Was the administration merely lucky?

The answer most likely lay in a principle that is always necessary for success, it seems, and that is the principle of perseverance. Pat Robertson, in his book *The Secret Kingdom* issued during this period, dwelt at length on this principle, which he described as a law built into the universe. "The ways of the universe yield to perseverance," he said, illustrating with the story of the egg and the chick, who has to keep pecking and pecking, working and struggling, to fight his way out of the place where he was conceived. Before long, he attains the strength to cope with a new life and breaks free of the shell.

"Certain risks," Robertson said, "go with new life and growth— the risks of freedom, we might say—but God prepares us for those risks, through perseverance and struggle, building our muscles, as it were, for each new phase. To refuse to struggle is to stand still, to stagnate."[7]

It was not likely that Reagan had philosophized his way through the matter of perseverance. Instead he had absorbed the principle from his patient, hard-working mother when he was a child and then developed it out of necessity at each stage of his ever-changing life's course. By the time he was president, at age seventy, he knew unconsciously the power of perseverance. He knew enough to "take what I can get" when dealing with legislators or political opponents, holding on for the time when he would obtain more. By using what he had and pressing on with it, he gradually received more, unconsciously applying another principle explored by Robertson, that of use: The one who uses what he has to the fullest, whether it be material goods or talents, will receive more and more.

A Virginia medical doctor unwittingly revealed a widespread perception of Reagan's persevering style in a casual political discussion a few months after midterm. "You can't go by what you see every day in the papers or on television," R. B. Henry of Norfolk said. "Day by day, he looks like he's in trouble and losing everything, but in the end he seems to get what he wants. I'd say he knows what he wants to do, he believes in it, and quite frankly he's gotten quite a bit done, even though that didn't always appear to be the case."

So it was with the economy, with strengthening of the military, and with regulatory reform.

However, with a number of other key proposals, immediate success could not be claimed. The so-called New Federalism, in which programs and tax bases to finance them were to be shifted over to the states, appeared to be making slow progress. The proposal to bring economic harmony and security to the Caribbean basin struggled against higher priorities. And little was heard of the high-sounding campaign goal to bind the three nations of the North American continent closer together, although Reagan and the other leaders continued to meet.

Even more serious to a large number of early backers of the conservative standard bearer was inaction on several social and moral issues that had wracked the nation spasmodically for years. Especially volatile were the questions of abortion and prayer in the schools.

Although many concerned with these issues—and similar ones like busing for school integration, tuition tax credits for children in private schools, and safety in the streets—had been willing to let economic concerns take priority, they were growing restless.

Reagan continued to insist that he would press such issues through to resolution, but he received little support within the establishment. Would he be able to deal with that establishment?

Questions also continued to arise about the Reagan administration's vision for the Middle East, specifically its commitment to the aspirations of Israel. In the quest for peace, would he go too far in making concessions to the Arabs?

At the same time, Central America threatened to erupt into a major conflagration, possibly embroiling the super powers. Some thought he was too harsh in his anticommunism, others not harsh enough.

Significant numbers of conservative leaders—politicians, writers, economists—reached a time of noisy discontent midway in Reagan's first term. Their writings and speeches often reflected a sense of betrayal by the president, deploring the so-called "pragmatism" they felt merely meant watering-down principle. Reagan's inclusion of a number of Republican establishment figures in the hierarchy—George Shultz, James Baker, David Gergen, and Richard Darman, and others at lower levels, especially in the State Department—was often at the center of their fire. This, they felt, typified a sell-out to the establishment. Some went so far as to label the administration's efforts as "neo-Carterism."

These critics from the right sensed a presidential weakening on tax cuts, the Communist threat in Central America, and aggressive Soviet conduct. And there truly were moments in 1981 and 1982 when such concerns seemed justified. The administration did seem to wallow, to ebb and flow with its convictions.

But those who became unduly alarmed had not really understood Reagan the man or Reagan the politician. They had missed a key fact: He is a man of principle, but he is a gradualist. He has on more than one occasion spoken variations of "it took the liberals fifty years to get us where we are and we won't get where we want to go overnight."

Again, it was the law of perseverance. Reagan did a lot of accommodating in 1982, and he did a lot of learning, but he remained confident that he would move his principles forward. The athlete in him often reflected that being president was like running a race—start strong, ease up a bit in the middle, and finish strong.

One television reporter was blunt in his assessment of this: "Reagan is a lot smarter than most politicians. He takes the long view. . . . He has that uncanny ability to know just what impact his actions will have. . . . That's why he can compromise."[8]

At any rate, the strong criticism of Reagan and his leadership diminished somewhat among the hardline conservatives, despite a loud hiccup over the appointment of Henry Kissinger to head a task force on Central America, as the administration ploughed into the final third of its term.

Part of this was attributable to an altered perception of Reagan, and part was due to the fact that matters did, indeed, change. But, again, it might have been that Reagan was simply picking up steam as he prepared to finish the race strong, having first begun strong and then eased up a bit.

The most obvious change was that the president no longer functioned only as the chairman of the board, although he did definitely remain the chairman. He also appeared to be serving increasingly as chief operating officer. He resisted the sort of attention to minute detail that many believed caused his predecessor to bog down and lose his idealistic thrust. But he became the central spokesman again—the articulator of the vision and the one who told how it was to be executed. In short, he became natural again. And he became more aggressive.

He also broadened his field of contact. He opened himself to more advisers. The most visible change was a steady increase in the influence of William P. Clark within the White House inner circle, which will be examined in detail in chapter 10. As national security adviser, Clark, described as one who knows the heart and mind of Reagan, gradually grew in stature and clout. Soon the Big Three of advisers— James Baker, Edwin Meese, and Michael Deaver—were the Big Four. Reports persisted that the group might have become narrowed to the Big Two—Baker and Clark—but that trend was not expected to last.

Whatever the case, Reagan's apparently increased firmness and vigor, especially in foreign affairs, might trace back to the office of Clark, who was known to think that Baker and others were at times too quick to compromise goals in order to govern. Clark, a fourth-generation rancher from California, with a reputation as a hard-liner, had the support of Reagan loyalists who distrusted Baker.[9] He would be one of those whom Reagan wanted at his side as he prepared to finish the race strong.

These White House modifications produced a crisper Reagan. Despite occasional lapses, he generally handled himself better in press conferences, although the mainstream newsmen seemed to deepen in their disrespect for his presidential leadership. He seemed better informed and more comfortable. His speechmaking, always more effective than the spontaneous give-and-take of press conferences because of the opportunities to prepare, showed greater poise and confidence. A national news magazine assessed these changes as follows:

> At times Reagan has seemed unfamiliar with important matters of state, and this has played into his critics' hands. An aide acknowledges that in the early months of his presidency, "issues were coming at him that he wasn't familiar with. His advisers may have been overprotective and too restrictive in the amount of information he received."
>
> Insiders insist that this is no longer so—that Reagan today is more deeply involved than ever before in day-to-day decisions—particularly in foreign policy. . . .

On domestic matters, the president had developed enough confidence that he no longer relied fully on staff recommendations. "He created his own options," said an aide.[10]

Still, the questions persisted. No amount of exposure seemed able to erase all doubts. How did this amateur citizen-politician, very different in every way from American leaders of the last fifty years, really think? Was he simply lucky? Was he really changing the tone and direction of the country? How were we to assess his rough-hewn faith in God? Was it significant for the rest of us?

★ ★ ★ ★ ★ ★ ★ ★ ★ ★ ★ ★ ★ ★ *3* ★ ★ ★ ★ ★ ★ ★ ★ ★ ★ ★ ★ ★ ★

The Divine Will

HELENE VON DAMM, U.S. Ambassador to Austria, who watched Ronald Reagan keenly from the vantage point of personal secretary for many years, said of him: "He has a strong belief that the Lord's will plays a part in the affairs of men and that faith in the Lord is essential."[1]

Frank van der Linden found in his biography of the former governor that "Reagan also felt 'called' to lead the nation, as ministers are 'called' to their congregations."[2]

Reagan himself said it this way in a letter to a woman with a handicapped son: "I find myself believing very deeply that God has a plan for each one of us. Some with little faith and even less testing seem to miss in their mission, or else we perhaps fail to see their imprint on the lives of others. But bearing what we cannot change and going on with what God has given us, confident there is a destiny, somehow seems to bring a reward we wouldn't exchange for any other."[3]

What are we to think about these presidential possibilities? What especially are we to think about them regarding this man, born 6 February 1911, in the little town of Tampico, Illinois, in a five-room flat in the general store on Main Street, this man who became the fortieth president of the United States and central figure of the free world? Does God have a plan for his life? Is it being fulfilled? Are these possibilities weird? After all, we're in the closing years of the twentieth century. The swirling philosophical currents of our time do not allow much room for the possibilities of a divine plan. Can we trust our national lives into the hands of one who believes God's hand is upon him?

To begin with, we should recognize that such old-fashioned thinking has far more proponents than we would surmise by reading the journals of our day, popular or intellectual. Nor do we accurately perceive the breadth of such thinking in the land if we depend upon television, either its news or its entertainment programming. No, we find such insight only among the people themselves, and not merely by a pass through a middle American main street. Such understanding is found in the homes, the churches, the offices, the fields, the factories, the places where people think a lot.

There you find folks who understand what Reagan means when he says, "I believe very deeply in something I was raised to believe in by my mother. I now seem to have her faith that there is a divine plan, and that while we may not be able to see the reason for something at the time, things do happen for a reason and for the best."[4]

George Gallup found in one of his surveys early in the eighties that 81 percent of Americans believe God has a plan for their lives.

It's significant to note the president's use of the word *now* in his remark about his mother. He has her faith *now*. Although he had learned much about the ways of God from his mother as the Reagan family hopscotched around northwestern Illinois—Tampico to Chicago's South Side, to Galesburg, to Monmouth, back to Tampico, and then "home" to Dixon—he did not immediately master them all. His thoughts about the will of God as a real-life concept were hammered out over many years through success and failure. That seems to be the biblical pattern for absorbing the teachings of the Almighty in light of the wilderness experience of the children of Israel and the painful struggles of the first followers of Christ.

So, by the time he was seventy, Reagan felt comfortable in speaking about the will of God—for his life, for the lives of others, and for the lives of nations. And millions of people, those who had also learned in the crucible of day-to-day life, apparently felt comfortable hearing him use such language. They were encouraged to find someone in high places who was able to articulate, in a manly way, some of their private inner thoughts.

Why then were significant numbers of opinion-makers unable to tolerate these views? Why did they snicker behind raised hands at the best of times, and snarl openly at the worst?

Saint Paul, a man of powerful intellect and broad worldly experience, had a good handle on the answer nineteen hundred years ago. The unspiritual person, he said, cannot accept the things of God. Indeed, such a person finds them foolish. He can't understand the grace, the gifts of God because such things are spiritually discerned and he, by his own choice, is unspiritual.[5]

This, carried to its logical conclusion, of course, means that godly reactions and perceptions cannot be expected from people who intentionally turn away from God. This is a truth that needs to be recognized by all. For example, it does no good for the serious-minded biblical Christian to roar angrily at the conclusions of the thoroughly secular-minded journalist or author or politician. More importantly, he should not imagine that a "conspiracy" lies behind every error in judgment. Plots do indeed surface from time to time, but usually the issue is ignorance.

In the discussions of Reagan and divine will, then, most opinion makers and takers simply were in the dark. The historical possibilities of Providence passed over their heads. That's why Frank van der Linden was so accurate when he wrote: "Despite his many years before the public, Reagan *has remained essentially a mystery* to many of his fellow Americans; and they are surprised to discover that he is deeply religious."[6]

Nelle Reagan, his mother, was a powerful influence on Ronald. She was of Scottish descent and an active member of the Disciples of Christ. Her faith was deep and stubborn. And it produced action. She was not merely pious. She worked out her faith—hard—carrying food from her skimpy cupboard to the hungry, visiting prisoners in jail, tending the sick. She believed in the divine will perhaps to the point of predestination, but she didn't believe this called for lying down and waiting for God to do it all. She saw herself as a fellow worker with God, which happened to be Saint Paul's view of the relationship, too.[7]

Unhappily, a high percentage of church leaders, as well as casual observers, today consider this "co-worker" concept to be presumptuous. They fail to see that God, in His sovereignty, has deigned to work with and through ordinary men to accomplish His will for the world, and He wants those men to stand up and be counted, to act boldly in His name.

Nelle Reagan understood. True, she was devout. But she was also tough.

An episode in Ronald's young life illustrates the care she took to transfer this toughness to him. He was the joy of her life, perhaps, but she wasn't going to pamper him.

Young Reagan, who preferred his father-bestowed nickname "Dutch" to what he felt was a sissy name, Ronald, was in the third grade during their stay in Monmouth. He fell victim to a bully, and life became miserable. The larger boy would beat him up each afternoon on the way home from school. When he could, Dutch would outrun him, and the bully would follow him all the way to the next door house.

"Boy, this bully would drive me home, day after day, and I'd be in tears," the president recalled. "One day, when I turned the corner and the bully was right there, having at me, I saw my mother standing there on the front steps.

"I thought, 'Oh, safety!'

"But she said, 'You can't come in the house until you turn around and fight him.'

"I was in tears but she said, 'Go back, you're not coming in here until you fight!'

" 'Oh, betrayed by my only friend!' I thought.

"So I turned around, waded in and threw a couple of punches, tears streaming down my face. To my surprise, the bully took off and ran, and that was the end of him. I learned a very good lesson."[8]

God's hand may have been on him, but it was necessary for him to work out his own salvation, as Saint Paul would have urged.[9]

The lesson with the bully plainly had an impact on Reagan that has been felt down to the present day and may even have touched his foreign-policy attitudes. For none would dispute he still has trouble abiding bullies, whether at the local or the international level.

It was not an entirely new phenomenon to have a man in the White House who believed in the concreteness of the will of God. Reagan's predecessor, Jimmy Carter, for example, possessed an understanding of the theological and historical truth that God touches and directs the lives and the affairs of men. While he never said, at least publicly, that God had "ordained" him to be president, he did nonetheless say, when pressed, that he had become convinced it was the Lord's purpose for him to run for election. "I've never asked God to make me President of the United States," he declared. "I pray only that God will help me to do the right thing." He believed that God's hand was upon him, that there was a divine will for him.

Lincoln, of course, was well known for his sense of the will of

God. As he left Springfield, Illinois, bound for Washington, "with a task before me greater than that which rested upon Washington," he said: "Without the assistance of that Divine Being who ever attended him, I cannot succeed. With that assistance I cannot fail. Trusting in Him who can go with me, and remain with you, and be everywhere for good, let us confidently hope that all will yet be well." Great suffering lay ahead. He foresaw it. But he knew that the hand of God was upon him and that he must move forward.

For those acquainted with the Bible—and the Gallup polling organization reports that nearly half of Americans read from the Bible every month—belief that God has a plan for individual's lives is commonplace. The Scriptures speak plainly to the point.

Paul the apostle, who may have been under confinement in Rome at the time, wrote these confident words to the Ephesians and others in the area: "We are his [God's] workmanship, created in Christ Jesus for good works, which God prepared beforehand, that we should walk in them."[10] He spoke plainly about not only the Creator but also man the creature. God had a plan for these people. His intention was for them to walk in it. They hadn't simply been brought forth and cast out into space willy-nilly. He had a plan, and it consisted of "good works."

David the king, a rough, tough warrior and leader of his people, wrote even more tenderly than Paul. In the soaring, majestic yet simple language of Psalm 139, he spoke this to God:

> For thou didst form my inward parts,
>   thou didst knit me together in my
>   mother's womb.
> I praise thee, for thou art fearful and
>   wonderful.
>   Wonderful are thy works!
> Thou knowest me right well;
>   my frame was not hidden from
>   thee,
> when I was being made in secret,
>   intricately wrought in the depths of
>   the earth.
> Thy eyes beheld my unformed substance;
>   *in thy book were written, every one*
>   *of them,*
>   *the days that were formed for me,*
>   *when as yet there was none of them.*[11]

Writing anthropomorphically and conjuring up images of little black books and the like, David made plain the truth that God has a plan for individuals. That plan, he said, is seen by God even before the birth of the person. Thus God can be said to have His hand on the lives of people. The additional truth that must be seen is that an individual can respond to that touch by God, walking purposefully and meaningfully under it, or he can ignore it, attempting to direct his own life.

God *wants* men to work in His will. It's the place of His provision, His prosperity. That's why He's gone to such great lengths to make it possible for them to do so. Paul explained that God wanted it so badly He took the burden of accomplishing it upon Himself. Indeed, the apostle wrote to one group of Christians, "God is at work in you" right now to cause them to *want* to do His will and also to be able to do it.[12]

He does it quite naturally, by the Holy Spirit, who Paul says is the only One who knows the thoughts of Almighty God. "Now we," he explains, "have received not the spirit of the world, but the Spirit which is from God, that we might understand the gifts bestowed on us by God."[13] That's how frail, weak human beings live in the divine will.

Actually it's accomplished when an individual determines he wants it to be. He can do very little about it on his own beyond desiring for it to happen. All he can do is throw himself upon God, which Paul referred to as presenting oneself "as a living sacrifice" through Jesus Christ. This, he explained, shatters the bonds of conformity that hold so much of the world in slavery and allows one to transcend that conformity as the Holy Spirit works through the mind to guide us toward God's will, His perfect plan for our lives.[14]

It is not weird. It is not strange. It is quite natural, according to the accounts found on the pages of the Holy Scriptures.

Therefore, significant numbers of people, far from being offended by the discovery that a political leader has a sense of God's will at work in his life and in the life of the country, are actually reassured. They understand. They may frequently falter themselves in their struggle with the problems of life, but they like the idea that someone of their kind bears responsibility for the affairs of their country.

When he was a candidate for president in 1976, Reagan wrote to a woman in Oklahoma, saying he had "come to realize that whatever I do has meaning only if I ask that it serve His purpose." He continued:

I believe that in my present undertaking, whatever the outcome, it will be His doing. I will pray for understanding of what it is He would have me to do.

I have long believed there was a divine plan that placed this land here to be found by people of a special kind, that we have a rendezvous with destiny. Yes, there is a spirit moving in this land and a hunger in the people for a spiritual revival.

If the task I seek should be given to me, I would pray only that I could perform it in a way that would serve God.[15]

The task was *not* given to him. He was defeated in his run for the GOP nomination. Still, the sense of God's call on his life remained. In 1980, he was saying the same things about God's having "a plan for each one of us."

Dee Jepsen, wife of United States Senator Roger Jepsen of Iowa, described an occasion when such awareness was very much before Reagan as he campaigned for the highest office in the land.

"My husband and I were traveling with Governor Reagan," she recalled. "I guess it was when we came back to the East Coast with him after a campaign trip, and I had the opportunity to slip over and sit by him for a second. I wanted to give him spiritual support because I know how much that means."

The tall, attractive wife of the Iowa Republican (she would one day serve in the White House as special assistant to the president for public liaison, dealing primarily with women's issues) was pensive for a moment. "It means more than anything else to me, when we're working and campaigning hard in a secular campaign and someone will come up and give you some spiritual support.

"So I just said, 'Governor'—because it was governor at that time—'I'd like to share something with you.' And I said, 'Well, I know you're a Christian—and we are too—and I just want you to know that we are praying for you, and I really believe God has raised you up for such a time as this, and He's going to use you greatly.' "

Recalling the moment three years later, Mrs. Jepsen smiled softly and her voice lowered ever so slightly. "And he had tears in his eyes, and he patted my arm and said, 'Aw—I can't thank you enough for all that; I really appreciate it.'

"And then I slipped back to my seat. And before we got off the plane, he came up and said, 'I just want to tell you how much I appreciate those prayers, because, you know, I can't pray to win.'

" 'No,' I said, 'but you can pray that God's will will be done.'

"And he said, 'Yes, I know. That's right. God's will.'

"And he was so visibly touched that I never had any question, if I ever did before—which I didn't—that he had a tender heart for the Lord. It was very obvious."

In 1981, Reagan was in the White House, as foretold in a simple modern-day prophecy in 1970. Considerable time has passed, some of it good, some not so good. Now what? What are we to make of these matters of faith in God and a divine will—in the White House?

The Growth of Faith

FROM EVERY CONCEIVABLE source the story was the same. Ronald "Dutch" Reagan had always been a nice, likeable guy. But I was looking for something deeper than that. Niceness and likeableness do not necessarily mean closeness to God. And that's what I was especially interested in. Assuming that the current President of the United States had a relationship with the Lord, what was its history? How had it taken shape?

As we've already noted, "Dutch," who received that nickname right after his birth when his dad said he looked like "a big, fat Dutchman," was deeply influenced by his mother. As a quiet child who spent a lot of time playing alone in his early years, he naturally grew accustomed to Nelle's remarks about the Lord. He fell right in with them and had no reason to disbelieve or dispute them. They came as naturally as breathing.

But Jack Reagan, his father, for all the strain he apparently caused the family from time to time because of his drinking and tendency to wander, was a strong moral influence on young Ronald, too. He particularly affected him in matters of racial and religious prejudice, which also blended into other questions of compassion and tolerance. In later life, Reagan often repeated an account illustrating his father's adamancy against discrimination.

It seems that Jack, working as a traveling shoe salesman, went into the only hotel in a small town one deep winter night.

"The clerk saw his name on the register," Ronald recalled, "and said, 'You'll like it here, Reagan. We don't let Jews in here.' "

Jack, a Roman Catholic in a Protestant age and region, picked up his bag with a few angry words and stormed out. "If you won't let Jews in, the next thing, you won't let Catholics in, and I'm a Catholic," he fumed.

With snow cascading down, he spent the night in his car and eventually wound up with pneumonia.

Dutch never forgot the episode and later did a similar thing himself regarding discrimination against some black players on his college football team. As he recounted it, the Eureka College team, for which he was a first-string guard, stopped overnight on a road trip not many miles from the Reagan home, but the hotel clerk would not let the three blacks on the team stay there. The coach, like Jack Reagan at an earlier time, was furious and wanted the team to sleep in the bus. But Dutch suggested he take the three players and himself to his house in a cab and spend the night. As one of the men recalled years later, "That sort of entrenched the friendship."

As noted earlier, incidents like these put flesh and bones on young Reagan's religious beliefs, as undeveloped theologically as they might have been at that early age. True, there were ebbs and flows in the evolution of those beliefs into a solid faith, yet they were never put away. Reagan, like everyone, simply had a lot of growing up to do.

First there was the typical small-town high school life to pass through and Reagan did it typically, playing football, swimming, and earning a more than moderate amount of recognition over the years for his lifeguard work at Lowell Park on the Rock River three miles outside of town. The first buds of the acting career that were to lead to Hollywood sprouted in those years as he performed, apparently admirably, in school plays.

He also fell in love with the preacher's daughter, Margaret "Mugs" Cleaver. Eventually, starting to grow tall and handsome by the time he was a senior, he won her affections and became her steady boyfriend.

Through those years and then on into Eureka College near Peoria, a school affiliated with the Disciples of Christ, Reagan continued to be known as a nice, likeable guy. He was quieter than his older brother, Neil, more popularly known as "Moon," but remained outgoing and friendly to all. There is little evidence of a special dynamism in his relationship with God. He went to church and took the rest more or less for granted. "Life is just one grand sweet song, so start the music," the motto read beneath his nickname in the high school yearbook. And that's the way it seemed to be.

In college, he walked in the same channels, pursuing a degree in economics and sociology, and thoroughly enjoying himself on the football field and the competitive swimming lanes. In addition to pressing on with an attraction to the stage and indeed steadily improving his skills, he dipped his foot into the political waters as a student strike leader against a cost-cutting proposal to eliminate a number of courses and teachers. His speechmaking in this cause was a smashing success, and he found he liked it.

He was also more than a little occupied in pursuit of Mugs Cleaver, who had also enrolled at Eureka. So he was busy and popular and healthy, notwithstanding an early-age need for eyeglasses. And he loved Eureka, showing forth clearcut evidences of the exuberance and optimism that would characterize him over the next fifty years.

For Reagan the graduate those experiences rolled together to lead him into five enjoyable and educational years as a radio sports announcer, first in Davenport, Iowa, and then in Des Moines. Blossoming quickly, he covered Big Ten football, Chicago major league baseball, swimming, boxing, track, everything. As for the Lord, well, He was there. Reagan knew it, but he was rather passive. He simply wanted— and took—everything God had for him.

Capitalizing on a trip to the West Coast to cover the Chicago Cubs in spring training, Reagan made contact with a former radio colleague who was singing with a band in Hollywood. From that came an introduction to an agent, a screen test, and ultimately a two-hundred-dollar-a-week movie contract. He was on his way as an actor, a career he would pursue for twenty-seven years. He spiced that up with an activist role in the Screen Actors' Guild, serving six terms as the union's president, which heightened his college-sparked inclinations toward political leadership.

With these activities, Reagan's contacts in the Hollywood community broadened and deepened. Respect for his leadership grew among many of the film celebrities of the fifties, and his role in leading SAG through the painful and confusing Communist-clouded years increased his public exposure. He was diversified. And he was respected. But his film career never reached the level for which he yearned, with one or two temporary exceptions.

One of the tragedies of this period that left its mark on the young, aspiring actor—and unquestionably flavored his attitudes toward many of the social problems he would encounter as a political leader—was the failure of his first marriage. He and Jane Wyman, the actress, were married in 1940 and became one of Hollywood's highly publicized "perfect" couples. In 1947, battered by twin careers, his zealous, hard work for SAG, and diverging personal tastes, that relationship fell apart. They were divorced in 1948, and Jane received custody of their eight-year-old daughter, Maureen, and three-year-old adopted son, Michael.

Reagan, by his own account, did not handle this failure well. He later wrote: "I suppose there had been warning signs, if only I hadn't been so busy. But small-town boys grow up thinking only other people get divorced. Such a thing was so far from even being imagined by me that I had no resources to call upon."[1]

He tried the Hollywood bachelor role again, with a Cadillac convertible, luxury apartment, and big income, but loneliness and unhappiness exceeded any enjoyment as a man-about-town. He was basically drifting. Where was that plan of God's?

"All of us, I suppose," he recalled later, "have a lonely inner world of our own, but I didn't want to admit to mine. My loneliness was not from being unloved, but rather from not loving.

"I wanted to care for someone," he said bluntly.[2]

Although his inner man was not developed well enough for walking through stressful times of that depth, he nonetheless, almost by rote, was able to turn to God for support. He knew enough to pray. He knew enough to hang on. But he didn't have the collective support that so many of us Christians fail to enlist, usually through lack of knowledge or embarrassment. The cliché for this support is "fellowship," spoken of at length in the Bible as necessary and a goal of the Christian experience.

A New Testament writer warned that believers ignored such fellowship at their peril as times got bad. "Let us consider how to stir up one another to love and good works," he said, *not neglecting to meet together,* as is the habit of some, but *encouraging one another,* and all the more as you see the Day drawing near."[3]

This was a point that would raise its head later in life.

But Ronald Reagan survived. His own experience, however, and that of his children would drive deep into him a churning concern for the home—for families, for children, for old-fashioned values.

"There is no easy way to break up a home," he reflected, "and I don't think there is any way to ease the bewildered pain of children at such times."[4]

It was a most significant time in the evolution of his faith, many miles and many lifestyles from the quiet streets of Dixon, Illinois. And it continued for four years, until he met and married a young actress named Nancy Davis. At that point his personal life took a sharp turn upward, reinforcing and stabilizing the values that had sounded easy in conversation but proved painful in life. "God and family" was becoming more than a catchy slogan for him.

The year 1954 was significant for Reagan, too. Its political ramifications were important, but first was the impact on him personally. That was the year he went to work for General Electric.

At first glance, coming on the heels of a declining film career and even a stab at Las Vegas show business, the G.E. move looked like another meandering step. But as is so often the case with individuals trying to follow the divine plan that they are persuaded exists, wandering eventually begins to take on the look of a pattern. David McCahon, a Boston business executive, expressed it this way: "At any given point, if you look behind you, you're likely to think your path is drifting aimlessly. It seems to be nothing but a series of twists and turns, crossing and overlapping with itself. But when it's run its course, and you begin to see it the way God does, it makes beautiful, logical sense."

Assuming the existence of God's plan for Reagan's life during that period, it operated at two levels, as is so frequently God's way. First, Reagan used his entertainer's skills as host of "General Electric Theater," which became television's leading Sunday night program. It featured major Hollywood stars in guest appearances, but Reagan was on the screen every week. His face and his voice became familiar to families all across America. The show was one those families could trust—clean, basically wholesome, entertaining. The same identity rubbed off onto the host.

But for the man of faith budding within the actor, the other phase of the job was probably more important. He was expected to tour G.E.'s 139 plants all across the land and to speak to their 250,000 or more employees. He was to come face to face with a cross-section of America. Cameras and screens were no longer there to mediate. He grasped hands and looked into eyes. His task was different from theirs, but he worked hard.

And, as I've suggested before, these were the people who had more concern about God than opinion-makers would have us believe. "They want the truth," Reagan said later. "They are friendly and helpful, intelligent and alert. They are concerned . . . and they are moral."[5]

This mixing with ordinary people was just what the midwesterner turned westerner needed. He was forced to remember that Hollywood the Tinseltown was not America; neither was the dream-maker at the opposite side of the continent, Madison Avenue. There was also Schenectady and there was Youngstown and there was Memphis. G.E. plants were located in thirty-eight of the states.

Increasingly, his boyhood experiences—the lessons learned from Nelle and Jack—were validated. So, too, were the soaring verses from one of the well marked passages in his mother's worn King James Bible, which he had heard so often:

> Who can utter the mighty acts of the Lord? who can shew forth all his praise?
> Blessed are they that keep judgment, and he that doeth righteousness at all times.
> Remember me, O Lord, with the favour that thou bearest unto thy people: O visit me with thy salvation;
> That I may see the good of thy chosen, that I may rejoice in the gladness of thy nation, that I may glory with thine inheritance.[6]

Throughout this period of developing convictions and understanding, Ronald Reagan was intensely private about his faith. If he was going to talk about God, he would have to know and trust the people to whom he was talking.

With Pat and Shirley Boone that relationship eventually developed as the two couples were thrust together numerous times at the school attended by their children. "We met them, I guess, the first at school," Pat recalled. "We had children in school at the same time."

The school was the John Thomas Dye School, a quaint private institution in the Bel Air hills. "So we met Ron and Nancy, along with a lot of other parents, including actors and actresses, and their kids," Boone said. "And we were at every school function and, after awhile, we saw that they were, too. They seemed to be really interested in the kids' activities and the school programs."

Common interests in the entertainment business and—they learned—in politics, especially conservative politics, soon had them talking together. "We'd stand around drinking this spiced tea, which is always a part of your John Thomas Dye events for the parents," Boone remembered. "There was this great big, walk-in fireplace, about six feet high, and it always had a roaring fire in it, and the parents would stand around bragging about their kids and complimenting each other, and talking about things."

Pausing for a moment to reflect on those times in the early sixties, first smiling and then growing serious, Pat continued: "And quite often we'd start talking about politics, or the government, and the way things were going, and he was always so impressive to me. . . ."

As for spiritual matters, the conversation began in a very low key. "It began very generally from the school," Shirley said, "because the school sort of had a spiritual status—a nebulous one, not church oriented or even religion oriented . . . but it was like a family."

Actually the spiritual discussions weren't really discussions, but rather occasional comments and references that made it evident to each of the two couples that they shared a common faith in God. They included references to prayer and thanksgiving.

Nonetheless, the conversations had enough content for the Boones to be convinced of the genuineness and sincerity of the Reagans' faith. The talk was tentative, general. But an evolution toward strength was obviously occurring.

Another important touchpoint in faith for Reagan was his relationship with the Rev. Donn D. Moomaw, senior pastor of the Bel Air Presbyterian Church. "I met him when I came here nineteen years ago," Moomaw recalled. "He was attending Bel Air Church—not too regularly, I guess, but he seemed to increase his attendance and became quite an active participant in the worship services."

Moomaw and Reagan fell into a good relationship on several grounds. First, the pastor was a college football All-American, big, unpretentious, straight-talking, and Reagan admired that. But the football player also knew how to preach the gospel, and he was an innovative church leader. Reagan admired that, too. It was only a matter of time before warm friendship developed into trust and freedom to talk openly.

"We became friends," Moomaw said late one afternoon in his church study, "more than just a pastor and a member of the congregation. There were times when we talked through different issues of faith and life." Observing pastoral privacy, he would not talk in detail about those issues, but it was clear that he was referring to profound matters of salvation, eternal life, the divinity of Christ, the will of God, plus the day-to-day problems of living that touch upon these broader theological matters.

Other growth occurred through the forum of debate, Moomaw related with a short chuckle. Sometimes it was by phone, sometimes in person. "He sometimes would call me after hearing a sermon," he said, "and we would talk about it." The implication of the pastor's tone was that Reagan did not always applaud Moomaw's sermons, but felt free to talk about them in terms of his own experience and the understanding that had been evolving over the years.

"He was very intelligent in his knowledge of the Scriptures," the pastor said.

On a more public level, Reagan was "always very attentive in worship," Moomaw recalled. "During a worship service, he became involved in the total experience—the sadness, the rejoicing, the singing," he said. "He was as alert to the full meaning of worship as anyone could be."

Interestingly, the pastor remembered that the man who was to become president was "quite demonstrative in his love of the great hymns." They obviously transported his early memories of such worship experiences with his mother into the present. The times had changed; the truth of the church's great songs had not.

Although he did not relate it that afternoon, it was reported by those who know both Moomaw and the Reagans that he once pressed Ronald as to whether he "knew" his salvation was assured.

According to the friends, Reagan replied, "Yes, I know."

"Why?" Moomaw reportedly asked.

"Because I have the Savior."

In a similar vein, Dr. Adrian Rogers of Memphis, a prominent Southern Baptist leader, told how he had pressed the same point. (This was, after all, the point for Christian leaders to press as Ronald Reagan, Jimmy Carter, and John Anderson—all professing Christians—lined up against one another in 1980.) "Governor Reagan said that his faith is very personal," Rogers related, "that God is real to him. He had a personal experience when he had invited Christ into his life."

According to his account, Rogers then asked Reagan a most pointed question: "Do you *know* the Lord Jesus or do you only know *about* Him?"

Rogers said Reagan declared, "I *know* Him."[7]

To evangelicals, the point is an important one. For, according to the Bible, it is not enough merely to believe intellectually that Jesus is the Son of God, the Messiah. To become a child of God, one must act on the understanding and "receive" or accept Jesus into one's life as Lord and Savior. Although taught by the overall flow of the New Testament, this is stated quite precisely by the apostle called John:

> To all who *received* him [the true light, Christ], who believed in his name, he gave power to become children of God; who were

born, not of blood nor of the will of the flesh nor of the will of man, but of God.[8]

Moomaw relates that Reagan had "readily admitted difficulty in being vocal about his faith." As with so many men—more so than women—of his generation, especially those leaning toward the rugged individualism rooted in American frontier days, ideas about God tend to be closely guarded. "It is so personal," Reagan told Moomaw.

The Bel Air pastor believed this difficulty didn't in any way suggest Reagan was ashamed of his faith in Christ or lacking in knowledge regarding it. It's something he "doesn't feel like talking about publicly and indeed does not feel able to talk publicly about."

"His faith is very pious and very personal," Moomaw said.

He was quick to point out, however, that Reagan's belief rests on more than personal feelings. "It's a knowledgeable faith," he emphasized.

During the years at Bel Air Church, Reagan revealed a developing knowledge about Scripture and about doctrine in particular. And it was a conservative view of doctrine, which was natural considering his youth and also the churches he attended in these maturing years, exemplified by Bel Air Presbyterian.

The process of faith development continued in Reagan's years as governor, according to accounts of people who were in positions to observe. Many of the events in that process were the kind that begin to add muscle and bone to any inner spiritual development that may have occurred. They also brought forth a more public proclamation of what he believed in the realm of God and godly conduct.

The first steps came immediately. Herb Ellingwood, who served with Reagan and then became special assistant attorney general of California in the following administration, recalled it this way:

"Inauguration week in January, 1967, provided some cautious optimism to Christians. This new governor . . . at a prayer breakfast stated: 'Belief in the dependence on God is essential to our state and nation. This will be an integral part of our state as long as I have anything to do with it.'

"In one of his inaugural addresses . . . Reagan concluded by quoting Benjamin Franklin: 'He who introduces into public office the principles of primitive Christianity will change the face of the world.' "[9]

Governor Reagan, besides the mammoth task of getting a new administration underway, faced a crisis right away. It involved the death penalty, specifically the execution of a man who had murdered a police officer.

"It was the toughest decision in my life," Reagan told Ellingwood after the latter became his adviser on executive clemency. "It's never easy to be the judge of a man's life or death."

The decision to go ahead with the execution "came after a lot of prayer," Ellingwood reported.

Increasing the visibility of his beliefs, Reagan asked Billy Graham to speak at a joint session of the California legislature. Members of the executive branch and the Supreme Court were invited to join the legislators, and all heard a clear challenge for them, as the political and governmental leadership, to be bold enough to lead California spiritually as well.

"That one event changed the lives of many in the state capital," Ellingwood recalled. "Some were officials, more were appointees, most were civil servants."[10]

During this time as governor, Reagan continued to meet from time to time with close Christian friends from outside the government like Moomaw and Boone. The Bel Air pastor would visit the Reagans at their Sacramento residence, and the Reagans also spent a lot of weekend time at their Pacific Palisades home, keeping the contact alive. A person close enough to both parties to be aware of private activities confided that Reagan and Moomaw occasionally discussed and prayed over the major political, moral, and ethical issues facing the administration.

The relationship with Boone was usually sustained during this period by brief bits of conversation managed at political or charitable functions. Boone remembered one such night in Palm Springs, as Reagan was finishing up his second year as governor. "I was asked to come down to introduce him at some fund-raising event. I don't think the dinner was even for him, but for Republican candidates or something. He was the main speaker and I was asked as a friend and supporter to introduce him. So we sat at the head table and had dinner together, and we got on some serious topics, with spiritual and moral overtones."

Sitting in his Beverly Hills home on a quiet Sunday night, Boone paused as he reached back eleven years to recapture the event. Interrupting his faraway gaze in the dimly lighted family room, he glanced at me. "He knows that—Shirley and I and Nancy and Ron often talked about spiritual things, so he knew this was important to us."

In those few minutes in Palm Springs, Boone and Reagan talked about the abortion issue, which was just beginning to rip at the state and which we will explore in chapter 5, and about the difficulties in holding onto principle while trying to govern a political entity. Being governor of such a diverse state was hard.

"But he felt they were gaining on things," Boone said.

"We always let him know that we prayed for him—the folks at our church—we prayed regularly for him and other officials by name. And I reminded him of that again. And he just let me know that the prayers were being answered."

After becoming president, Reagan was caught in the situation that has proved so difficult for others. How does such a public figure—so recognizable, so powerful—participate in any kind of worship in public gatherings without destroying it for others as well as himself? Leaders, in this country and others, have wrestled with this for centuries.

Reagan at first combatted the problem by refraining in general from attending public church services, in contrast to his predecessor, Jimmy Carter. Deciding against services conducted especially for the White House, as held frequently by Presidents Nixon, Johnson, and others, he depended almost entirely on his private devotions. However, presumably with strong encouragement by Moomaw and others, the president after three years was determined to find ways to attend church in Washington, despite the risks, and plans were afoot to make that possible. Earlier, Moomaw had felt that experimentation was called for. "A president must be willing to try different things to go to church," he said. "The inhibitions to public worship can be overcome—and indeed *should* be overcome."

At any rate, Reagan remained rather quiet about the Lord and matters having spiritual overtones for the first year or more of his administration. This was dictated in large part by his political agenda, centering on economic and budgetary matters, and by the changes in his environment.

In private, however, he had periodic fellowship and his dependence upon God grew. Moomaw, Boone, Billy Graham, Cardinal Cooke of New York, Mother Teresa of India, and others—plus his wife, Nancy—provided opportunities for spiritual deepening.

I asked Moomaw if he still had contacts with the president now that he is in Washington. "We have some conversations," he said. "And when we do see each other, we span time very fast because we've been through some emotional occasions together," suggesting that they often move quickly from chit-chat to serious conversation about whatever subjects may be confronting them. A source familiar with the activities of both men made it plain that the president has continued his practice of seeking spiritual input from Moomaw (as well as others) about certain matters he faces. The implication was that this consisted primarily of prayer and discussion of broad spiritual principles, rather than direct policy advice.

Questioned as to his continuing contacts with the president, Boone said, "Though our meetings are usually brief, and far between now, we do see that there is [spiritual] growth and that he still—there is still that great, pragmatic, practical approach, even though he's obviously not at this stage of the game going to sacrifice his principles."

Boone's reference to growth supported a belief by a number of close observers that Reagan, after a quiet start, had been showing a certain maturation in his utterances regarding spiritual, biblical principles as his administration moved through the second half of its term. His statements about abortion, prayer in the schools, families, and the like seemed sharper, more consistent. His delivery of them, these observers felt, revealed a deep, yet calm, sincerity.

I asked Moomaw if he felt Reagan was maturing in his Christian life. "I would not call it maturing," he replied, "but rather that he is becoming freer and more vocal."

After all, he noted, Reagan's Christian roots go way back, producing, not a schooled and sophisticated faith, but a common, down-to-earth one. It's simply showing more, Moomaw concluded.

The significance of this surge in the evolution of Ronald Reagan's faith to the time in which we live will become increasingly clear as we explore the condition of the country and the world. It will drive right to the edge of the thicket surrounding one of this book's major questions: Can he govern?

Before we can leave this hopscotching examination of the development of a man's faith, we must deal with a point that surfaces at least annually before the general public, and one that is debated far more often than that by serious-minded Christians. Why does Ronald Reagan seemingly give so little of his substantial income to church work or other charities?

Even "Doonesbury's" creator, Garry Trudeau, turned his stinging wit upon the subject in a commencement address at Harvard. Why, he wondered, did President Reagan give away only three thousand dollars of the half-million he made the previous year?

Those Christians who believe that tithing—giving 10 percent—is the minimum appropriate evidence of commitment were asking the same thing on the basis of stories about Reagan's tax returns. In fact, the stories were an embarrassment to those among them who wanted desperately to be supportive.

A long-time associate of Reagan who has been in a position from time to time to know about such details said the explanation was simple, although not one to be accepted by the skeptical nature often required by newsmen, and thus not one that is offered.

The explanation went this way: Reagan gives varying sums to needy individuals or groups and simply doesn't deduct them because he believes such giving, according to biblical principles, is best done privately and without publicity. Often, too, the recipients—such as ordinary individuals in need or unincorporated groups—do not qualify for making such deductions on income tax returns.

This account regarding nondeductible gifts for individuals squares with a report stemming from his radio announcing days. Apparently Reagan, following the principle of tithing as taught him by his mother, sent 10 percent of his income to his brother, Neil, who was working his way through college. It seems his mother had taught him to be more concerned about giving than deducting.

Whether this explanation will satisfy critics today is uncertain. But that is only one of Reagan's several problems, as we will see.

★ ★ ★ ★ ★ ★ ★ ★ ★ ★ ★ ★ ★ ★ 5 ★ ★ ★ ★ ★ ★ ★ ★ ★ ★ ★ ★ ★ ★ ★

An Evolution of Politics

For Reagan the politician, 27 October 1964, was pivotal. Up to that point, he had been a pretty good actor, a good television host, a rousing dinner speaker, and a motivating company spokesman. From that point, he was the favorite son of American conservatives, a political leader of increasing magnitude.

That was the night of his nationwide television address in support of the Republican presidential candidate, Barry Goldwater, the night when even the skeptics were impressed. Goldwater was later trounced soundly by Lyndon Johnson, and most politicians figured the conservatives had been buried for keeps. But they had underestimated Reagan's impact with his basic, workaday, conservative themes delivered in the warm, sincere manner that was to become his hallmark. Lines from that Goldwater speech were capable years later of bringing tears to the eyes of the hard-line faithful:

—"This is the issue of this election: Whether we believe in our capacity for self-government, or whether we abandon the American revolution and confess that a little intellectual elite in a far-distant capital can plan our lives for us better than we can plan them ourselves.

—"A government can't control the economy without controlling people. And . . . when a government sets out to do that, it must use force and coercion to achieve its purpose.

—"Government does nothing as well or as economically as the private sector of the economy.

—"They say we offer simple answers to complex problems. Well, perhaps there is a simple answer—not an easy one, but a simple one—

if you and I have the courage to tell our elected officials that we want our national policy based upon what we know in our hearts is morally right.

—"You and I have a rendezvous with destiny. We will preserve for our children this, the last best hope of man on earth, or we will sentence them to take the last step into a thousand years of darkness."

In that half-hour talk, he laid out the criticisms against governmental trends in the United States that would form the skeleton of his discontent for the next sixteen years.

He spoke against what he considered to be Federal encroachment into the social fabric of the country, listing certain aspects of farm programs, urban renewal, public housing, welfare spending, unemployment programs, Social Security as it was structured, and compulsory medical activities. He criticized what he perceived as the hypocrisy of the United Nations and the harmful and wasteful nature of much of the foreign aid program. He was especially critical of stances that he thought showed lack of determination by the United States against international opponents.

With that stand, Ronald Reagan from Dixon, Illinois, showed forth his swing from Roosevelt liberalism as embraced by his father, Jack, in the dark days of the thirties to the Republican conservatism that had lain dormant since the reluctant days of Calvin Coolidge. He saw himself as one of the ordinary working people, even though he had passed into millionaire status and did little ordinary work beyond chopping wood and working around his ranch. "If I have a rapport with them," he said later, "it's because I'm one of them. I know what they believe in—family life and religious fiber, safe streets, and social order—the ideals that made this country great."[1]

That meant he wanted to "get the government off their backs," a phrase that would mark his speeches for a decade and a half.

The evolution of Reagan the politician seems perfectly logical as we stand on this side of the 1964 landmark, although, as noted in looking at his evolution as a man of faith, the path would not have been so plain as the transition was occurring.

A number of factors stand out. For example, as he prospered after World War II he paid more and more to the government in taxes.

This troubled him. It wasn't merely that he may have been a trifle greedy, but rather that he felt himself more and more asking the question of why one should work harder if he has to give half or more of his earnings away. It was a common complaint, especially within the motion picture community.

Again, we see here an illustration of a man's principles being hammered out by his personal experiences. Increasing taxes began to pinch him, and he developed a permanent opposition to income taxation—redistribution of wealth—as a way to run a country.

His union experience, especially in the battle to thwart a Communist takeover of Hollywood professions, also molded him for the future. Had he not been so directly involved, he probably would not have grown so quickly hostile to the workings of Marxism. But he soon became certain that Communism was one of the great threats to the freedoms he had since childhood taken for granted.

Roy Rogers and Dale Evans, the former Hollywood actors, were among those who through the activities of the Screen Actors' Guild saw the impact of those days upon Reagan's thinking. "I met him several times during the Second World War and after," Dale recalled, "and I always found him to be so straightforward with what he had to say. He wasn't given to a lot of small talk. But he made an impression even then of being a very nice man, and then he really got onto the free enterprise system. He knew it, and he really believed it."

Sitting in their offices above the Roy Rogers and Dale Evans Museum in the high desert country of Victorville, California, Dale could not resist a digression regarding the shaping of Reagan's marketplace views. "As far as I'm concerned," she said, "Jesus gave us a terrific example of the free enterprise system in the parable of the talents, and in other places, and I think this is what Ronald Reagan believes."

Her digression was illuminating. For in the parable a master rewarded the servants who took money left in their charge and worked with it, doubling it before the master returned. A third servant, who took the money left to him and hid it for safekeeping because he was afraid, received blistering condemnation from the master.[2]

Pat Robertson, in his book *The Secret Kingdom,* describes this parable as the centerpiece of what he calls the Law of Use, which is climaxed by Christ's universal principle: "To everyone who has will more be given, and he will have abundance; but from him who has not, even what he has will be taken away."[3] To Robertson—and to Reagan—this means that God wants people to use boldly that which they've been given—to work with it, creatively, experimentally, and to multiply it, not once but many times.

"Despite our preconceived attitudes . . . ," Robertson says, "God's Law of Use controls the ultimate distribution of wealth."[4]

That is the principle Dale Evans and Roy Rogers saw taking root in their friend so many years ago. Dale especially remembered a Saturday afternoon in Charlotte, North Carolina, when she and Reagan addressed a gathering of business people.

"He was one of the speakers ahead of me," she said. "And the people absolutely went wild over Ronald Reagan because that's what he spoke on—the free enterprise system."

"Yes," Roy jumped in, "we liked what we saw and what we heard. As I said, we didn't know him real well—you know, as a close friend or anything like that—but we knew him in the Screen Actors' Guild, and he made a lot of sense."

Perhaps the most significant steps in this early political development were taken in his job with General Electric. Not only did he develop a feeling for the faith and hope of the working people to whom he was exposed in the plants across the land, but he also absorbed much of the perspective of business and industry regarding conditions in the country and the world. Since his youth he had from afar viewed business and industry as the economic fulcrum supporting American life. But then from 1954 to 1962 he was thrust into position to begin to view life from the perspective of both business and industry. This did not give birth to his opinions but rather tended to help shape them as he articulated in a manner, like any good actor, to please and be understood by his audience.[5]

His speechmaking evolved from anecdotes about the movie industry and his own life to statements, often in answer to questions, about governmental growth, inflation, and individual freedom. International problems did not escape his broadening horizons either, especially in matters of U.S. defense.

It is important for those who wish to understand Ronald Reagan and his thought processes that they not be lured into viewing him as one who changed his political opinions to suit the times. Those opinions had been growing within him since the early postwar years. No, the changes were in his comfort with speaking about them publicly and in the power of growing conviction.

A stubborn earnestness and smiling sincerity had marked his life since childhood, taking flower rather dramatically in his college days and bursting into predominance in his SAG leadership. If Ronald

Reagan is anything, he is sincere. Friends and foes agree on this point. The General Electric days polished that sincerity to a luster that brightened television sets across the country when he made his last-ditch appeal for the election of Barry Goldwater over Lyndon Johnson.

The course was set. All that remained was for a handful of materially powerful men to recognize it and remove the obstacles, primarily financial, that lay in the way.

Reporter Frank van der Linden recalled it like this:

> Reagan looked like a knight in shining armor to three rich Southern Californians who were seeking just such a hero to rescue the Republican party from ruin: Holmes Tuttle, a Los Angeles Ford dealer; Henry Salvatori, founder of the Western Geophysical Company; and A. C. [Cy] Rubel, chairman of the board of the Union Oil Company. They felt sure that the genial actor, with his gift for plucking the heartstrings of the average American via television, could be built up into a credible candidate for governor of California.[6]

After numerous meetings and several hard-nosed confrontations, Reagan was committed by the spring of 1965 to seek the governorship. His rich supporters opened a "Friends of Ronald Reagan" office in Los Angeles, professional political management was secured, a successful mail appeal was launched, and the views of the Illinois-to-Iowa-to-California conservative were ready to compete.

It must be remembered that not everyone fell into line. The opposition was vehement. His friends may have seen him as the most effective spokesman for free enterprise in several generations, but a sizable number considered him to be a genuine threat to modern America and perhaps to the world. And many of the latter had benefited from the practical experience of holding power during the generally liberal era spanning from the depression thirties to the aberrant sixties. They had grown sophisticated in the use of power. And they did not take this new oldtimer seriously. He was an actor, after all.

Even the Hollywood crowd was slow to respond, with a few significant exceptions. Many of the big-name actors had become closely identified with the Democratic party, and those bonds did not break easily.

Pat Boone remembered those days, for they were the ones during which he and Shirley became well acquainted with Ron and Nancy through their children's school. "I said to Shirley several times, 'Boy, it's a shame a man like that—who thinks the way he does and speaks the way he does, as forceful and knowledgeable as he is—doesn't run for office,' " he recalled. "But we figured that was impossible— you know, an actor, that would never happen. And eventually when he did declare his intentions to run for governor and everybody was making jokes about it, we knew him well enough and felt his convictions were sound enough—we knew it was not just a 'Gee, I think this is a role I'd like to play'—I decided I would campaign for him. I felt he would make a great governor. I didn't know if he had a chance, but I was going to campaign for him."

Boone paused in the quiet of that Sunday evening in his home and his famous smile broke forth. "I laughed about it at that time, in the early stages, because there were only about three people in the entertainment business who would openly come out in favor of him and campaign and speak for him." He paused again. "Wendell Corey, Victor Jory, Piper Laurie and Pat Boone. Laurie, Corey, Jory, and Boone. It was the funniest thing. Eventually Roy and Dale and some others helped out, but the Democrats and Governor Pat Brown had every other entertainer on their side. All they had to do was name one and he'd show up.

"Of course, the next time around, after four years, it became the 'in' thing then, you know. Not that everybody made a wholesale switch, but these guys that were known to be Democrats said, 'Hey, we've got a great governor here,' and they campaigned for him."

As for the general political body in the nominating and electing process culminating in 1966, the most notable point to remember is that Ronald Reagan's opponents underestimated him, as they would fourteen years later. Their insistence on thinking of him as an actor— not taking him seriously—spelled defeat. His political evolution had progressed much further than they realized. Furthermore, the endless traveling and speaking for G.E. had taught him more about campaigning, with its long days and quick changes, than many politicians learn in a lifetime. He knew how to work hard and yet conserve energy. He knew how to relax and enjoy himself. And he knew how to use the media, especially television.

In 1966, contrary to the predictions of conventional wisdom, he defeated incumbent Brown by nearly a million votes. And four years later, after a controversial term, he was re-elected by about half that margin.

Reagan, of course, was thrust into the forest of wide-ranging issues and problems growing in any big, diverse state like California. He won some battles—and he lost some. Welfare reform was central, as was the transformation of a budget deficit into a surplus. Especially significant for the purposes of this book was the number of issues touching directly or indirectly on various aspects of family life and morality that came before his administration in rather quick succession. We saw in the previous chapter how these issues worked their way into a primary position in Reagan's Christian thinking through events and circumstances shaping his early and middle life.

Herb Ellingwood, who was in a position to watch closely, reflected on the human difficulties that rolled in upon the Governor to affect his leadership. "I have watched tears come to his eyes and listened as he choked for words when the two of us talked about the problems of the modern family. It sounds terribly sentimental; were that to happen in public, most would say he was only acting."[7]

Here's the way Reagan came down on those family issues, providing clues for conduct on a national scale a decade and a half later.

—He favored repeal of the inheritance tax. "It's important for parents to be able to pass on to their children the fruit of their labor," he said.

—He opposed busing of school children. "It disrupts family and neighborhood life without improving the quality of education," he argued.

—He advocated a requirement that parents be notified before their children could attend sex education classes.

—He favored private schools, including Christian schools. He felt that "the competition is good for the public school system, and parents should have that freedom of choice."

—He criticized any welfare provisions that encouraged fathers to be absent from the home.

—He opposed the application of the minimum wage to youth. His contention was that it prevented employers from hiring young, inexperienced people.

Ellingwood recalled that Reagan kept insisting that families should be the foundation of the nation. "Families—not government programs—are the best way to make our cultural and spiritual heritages perpetuated, and our values preserved," he quoted from the governor's remarks. Practicing this belief at the office, Reagan reportedly kept telling his cabinet staff not to work hours that properly belonged to their families. His success with this admonition, however, was mixed, by all accounts.

Listening to Reagan talk about family issues, a number of observers—some hostile, others merely questioning—raised doubts about his sincerity on such matters in light of relationships within his own family. Some felt he had not been especially close to his own children, for example—particularly those from his first marriage, Maureen, and Michael, who was adopted. By his own account, Reagan did not handle his divorce from Jane Wyman well. She received custody of the children and he went back to the bachelor life.

A close friend and colleague, asked specifically about reports of occasional difficulties in relationships with the children, denied knowledge of strains. But he added, "What can one do? The divorce, the broken home, it's hard. I think he did everything he could."

This friend felt Reagan had probably had a better relationship with all his children than his critics suggested, although there had been pain and suffering traceable to the divorce. As for the children from the second marriage, Patti and Ron, he disputed suggestions of familial strain or parental inadequacy. He noted, however, that all the offspring were "very much their own people."

As with many thoughtful governmental leaders, abortion was an especially difficult matter for Reagan. While governor, he signed legislation liberalizing an old California law. And, although he thought he had acted correctly, the legislation did not turn out well and he feels he erred. He still has a hard time acknowledging the error publicly.

It's necessary to remember the bitterness of the struggle at that time and the fact that Reagan had not been forced by circumstances to come to grips with all the realities of the abortion issue. Many of us who were faced with writing editorial positions on the matter in those early days understand his problem. It's one thing to think generally and quite another to get down to specific details and individual circumstances.

The new California legislation was worded to permit abortion in cases of rape or incest or in cases where the life of the mother was clearly threatened. After much agonizing, Reagan found himself impressed by the "self-defense" aspect. "I personally believe that termination of a pregnancy is the taking of human life and can be justified only in self-defense," he said.

He apparently genuinely felt that the legislation would overrule all other grounds, such as indications that a child would be malformed and handicapped.

The genuineness of that belief seems to be found in a brief exchange over dinner with his friend Boone during this period. Deploring the difficulty that political and governmental leaders have in trying to please their constituencies and simultaneously do what they believe to be right, he smiled into Boone's face and said, "But I believe I got a little pat on the back from the good Lord."

As the conversation was reconstructed by Boone after many years, he went on to explain: "This abortion thing—I haven't had to confront that till just recently. It was just not a part of my life. It's become a volatile issue. And I didn't have any clearly worked-out thoughts except that I just felt it was wrong, except perhaps in the case of women who've been raped or maybe when a woman's life is actually in danger, where it might be her life or this child's. And I didn't really know what to think about the cases where the doctors think there is a very good chance that the child will be born badly deformed. And I was still trying to work that out in my mind and decide which side of that issue to come down on. I wanted to do what was right and make up my own mind and not do what seemed politically expedient.

"I knew which side would be more popular with the majority of voters, so I prayed about it and thought about it and I had to make a decision on a certain day.

"So I made my decision and I came into the office and I told my legal aide that I had made my choice—that I would as governor be opposed to abortion on any grounds except rape or when a woman's life is threatened and that I would oppose abortion even if there was a very good likelihood that the child might be born deformed. I didn't think that we should play God and take that life into our own hands.

"It was a difficult decision, but I made it and came in and announced my decision.

"Then my aide—we were alone in the office—said, 'Governor, I thought you might like to have this,' and he handed me a painting. I don't know a lot about painting, but I looked at this and it was nice but nothing really special. So I said, 'Why do you want me to have this?'

"And he said, 'Well, I thought you'd like this particularly in view of the decision you've just made, because this painting was painted by a man who was born with no arms.'

"I looked at the painting again, and he told me the man had put the brush in his mouth and painted. He was living a successful, fulfilling, happy life even though he'd been born deformed.

"Well, I got goosebumps, and I just felt like the Lord was telling me I had made the right choice."

Many millions would agree that the governor had made the right choice regarding the deformity danger and the question of one human's trying to play God regarding another human life. But despite his conviction on that part and the fact that he had attempted to remain sensitive to the people, to morality, and to the leading of the Lord, the legislation was eventually twisted to such a degree that the abortion floodgates were opened in California. It proved easy for lawyers to convince the authorities that the emotional and psychological stress of bearing an unwanted child was tantamount to threatening a woman's life.

Those in a position to know Reagan's feelings say he has suffered greatly over the increase in abortions that eventually resulted from the California legislation when his intention had been the opposite.

And so it went with the evolution of Ronald Reagan the politician and government leader.

Welfare reform was probably the crowning achievement of Reagan's two terms as Governor of California and typified his concerns about governmental growth, inefficiency, and waste. It's particularly noteworthy in tracing the development of the onetime Roosevelt liberal to full-fledged Republican conservative. It further pointed to positions that would be manifest at the Federal level.

Lou Cannon, who covered Reagan from the beginning of his political career, provided a summary of the law that was hammered out in a remarkable bit of cooperation between the administration and the legislature:

> The California Welfare Reform Act is Reagan's proudest achievement in the eight years of his governorship. By almost any yardstick—liberal, conservative or managerial—the law has been a success. It is easier to administer than the law it replaced, and it pays AFDC (Aid to Families with Dependent Children) recipients more money. However, many who applaud the results of the legislation also believe that Reagan ascribes to it wonder cures which never occurred. The welfare reform bill tightened eligibility in several ways and reduced the number of hours an unemployed father could work and still have his family eligible for aid. Household furnishings were for the first time counted as assets. A complex and confusing "needs standard" was simplified into a uniform statewide schedule which varied

only according to family size. A one-year residency requirement, long advocated by Reagan, was written into law despite warnings that it was probably unconstitutional. Antifraud measures included a state cross-check between county welfare records and employer earnings records and financial incentives to counties to recover support payments from absent fathers. Grants were substantially increased. The family of three which had been getting $172 a month at the beginning of the year received $235 after the cost-of-living increase and passage of the welfare plan. And Reagan's pet demonstration project, the Community Work Experience Program, was introduced in some counties, requiring fathers and AFDC mothers without young children to work at public service jobs.

Both the Reagan administration and the Democratic legislative leadership had pledged to reform the welfare system, and both sides had something to crow about. The welfare rolls started to decline immediately. Within three years the AFDC caseload dropped from a high of 1,608,000 to 1,330,000. The efficacy of Reagan's welfare reform became a national article of faith among conservatives, and even among some who did not rally to the conservative banner.[8]

But a conservative he remained, strengthening in his convictions day by day. Government had become the master, not the servant, of the people. Its liberalism, often appearing so good and humane, was frequently cruel. Fiscally, it had become insane. Internationally, it was failing the world.

Jeffrey Hart, a social critic and writer who worked for both Richard Nixon and Ronald Reagan, describes Nixon as "the critical transition" between Eisenhower and Reagan. Without Nixon the Republican party, let alone the nation, would not have been ready for the conservative. For between 1952 and 1980, the GOP shifted its base from the Northeast to the Sun Belt and from WASP to a mixture of Southerners, ethnics, wealthy, laborers, intellectuals, and Archie Bunkers.[9]

In 1968, certainly, and also in 1976, the stage had not quite been set for Reagan to win the nomination. His evolution was still in process; so was the GOP's. Indeed, so was the country's.

By 1980, the transition was complete.

Boone, a politically active Californian, provided a bit of behind-the-scenes flavor regarding the final surge of that transition. It came in 1976, the year everyone thought political life was over for Reagan the aging conservative. "I remember when I was a Reagan delegate at the convention," he recalled, "and Gerald Ford was seeking and obtaining the nomination—that Reagan came within a whisper, a few votes, of becoming the nominee, but he didn't get it.

"I was there in Kansas City and went around and spoke to the Mississippi delegation and then to the New York delegation and did whatever I could to try to get more votes—and we did get more—but it just wasn't enough. And the New York guys said later, 'You know when Reagan walked into that room, people stood up.' They didn't know what to expect, and hadn't been exposed to Ronald Reagan. He didn't try to twist their arms. He spoke very matter-of-factly and said, 'These are the things that we believe together'—not from notes or anything—and you could almost see them saying together, 'This ought to be our guy.' "

But he wasn't the guy. The time had not come, despite the matter of age and the economic deterioration of the country.

Even so, on the night of Ford's acceptance speech, evidence of the transition identified by Hart was visible. The Ford demonstration was going on down on the floor of the convention and Reagan and his people had taken seats high in the upper balcony. Someone spotted Reagan and pointed up. Others looked up and pointed, and then others. Before long, it seemed that the whole convention was looking up. Cheers began. Television commentators thought it was just convention euphoria. But the applause and cheering didn't stop. Soon it was embarrassing—to Ford, to his people, and to Reagan. It was more than euphoria.

"I was down there," Boone said, "and there was this overwhelming feeling that said, 'This is supposed to be our man. What have we done? He's been gallant, he's been a gentleman, he's supported all our candidates and all our causes, even now, even though we've spurned him and gone to Gerald Ford.' There was this very emotional feeling there on the floor."

Boone went away from the convention mumbling to himself about what he had just seen, about the prophetic prayer that had been spoken in 1970 regarding Reagan and the White House, about Reagan's age.

"I pondered that [1970] prayer time," Boone said, "and I quite frankly asked, 'What was that all about?' I had thought Reagan was being prepared for something beyond the governorship, but at that moment I felt he obviously was not going to be president."

Age or not, the answer to Boone's question was simple: The transition had not been completed—for Reagan, for the Republican Party, or for the country. But circumstances and the Democratic Carter

Administration took care of the last part, and Reagan himself went to work on the first two.

Indeed, the transition from the defeated Ford to the victorious Carter was still underway when Reagan took his first steps to broaden the appeal of his party, to prepare it for its next encounter with the Democrats. Those steps, little noticed by anyone but conservatives at that point, came at a banquet of the Intercollegiate Studies Institute on 15 January 1977.

"The new Republican party I envision," he said, "will not, and cannot, be limited to the country club big business image that for reasons both fair and unfair it is burdened with today. It is going to have room for the man and woman in the factories, for the farmer, for the cop on the beat, and the millions of Americans who may never have thought of joining our party before. If we are to attract more working men and women, we must welcome them, not only as rank-and-file members but as leaders and as candidates."

He intended to try to lead the party into a new majority, a coalition reviving memories of his former political idol, Roosevelt, an alliance that would specifically include people with problems of inflation and unemployment, one very definitely embracing black people, who had for so long been given short shrift by the GOP.

To accomplish this, he said, "We have to find the tough, bright young men and women who are tired of the clichés and the pomposity and the mind-numbing idiocy of the liberals in Washington."

For those who were willing to hear, he pointed directly to the 1980 campaign that this "new" party would wage:

> We, the members of the new Republican party, believe that the preservation and enhancement of the values that strengthen and protect individual freedom, family life, communities and neighborhoods, and the liberty of our beloved nation should be at the heart of any legislative or political program presented to the American people.
>
> The United States must always stand for peace and liberty in the world and the rights of the individual. Given that there are other nations with potentially hostile design, we recognize that we can reach our goals only while maintaining a superior national defense, second to none.
>
> When we are maligned as having little thought or compassion for people, let us denounce the slander for what it is. Concern for the people is at the very heart of conservatism. Concern for the dignity of all men; that those in need shall be helped to become independent—not lifetime recipients of a dole; concern that those who labor and produce will not be robbed of the fruit of their toil

or their liberty. Concern that we shall not forfeit the dream that
gave birth to this nation—the dream that we can be as a shining
city upon a hill.[10]

Under that banner he began his work. He hadn't fully committed
to seeking the presidency in 1980, but neither was he ready to hang
up his conservative running shoes. Divine destiny was not his to execute, but it did seem to continue to hang there. For the moment,
however, his task was to reshape his party, and that he did. There
were struggles with the Ford people, with the Republican National
Committee, with other elements of the establishment. But steadily
the party broadened its vision to embrace most of the popular spectrum
and to exploit the increasingly conservative drift of the public mood.
The international and economic convulsions of the Carter years made
the task easier.

By the second quarter of 1978, Reagan was ready to run, but he
remained publicly uncommitted. His political evolution had run its
course—although there would be modifications, compromises, and
times to wait. Nonetheless, the principles were fixed, the speeches
were polished, the ad libs were ready. They had been tried at every
kind of banquet table imaginable and in his syndicated newspaper
column and radio show reaching into small towns all across the land.
Some experts said his positions blended common-sense conservatism
with a genuine concern for people. Others said he was dangerously
simplistic and short on details.[11]

What he was seeking, he said as the decade ended, was a return
to the days of stable prices, low unemployment, a sound dollar, and
competitive goods. He rejected conventional acceptance of shortages
of energy and other resources. He was confident that fiscal and economic wisdom would restore productivity, creativity, and prosperity
that would in turn open new vistas for raw materials and their use.

Central to his plans was an income tax cut for individuals and
businesses of 30 percent over three years, plus balancing of the Federal
budget, points that would haunt him painfully. Citing waste and fraud,
he called for massive reduction in Federal spending while seeking to
raise defense expenditures. And he was determined to reduce and
streamline Federal regulation.

Those were the Reagan broad strokes. He had reached the point
where he believed he could execute them. The evolution of his faith

had come a long way. So had the evolution of his politics. A significant number of people recognized this and believed he could execute the broad strokes and the little ones, too. So they elected him President of the United States on 4 November 1980.

Still the questions hang in the air: Can a man of his faith and political persuasion govern in our chaotic times?

★ ★ ★ ★ ★ ★ ★ ★ ★ ★ ★ ★ ★ ★ *6* ★ ★ ★ ★ ★ ★ ★ ★ ★ ★ ★ ★ ★ ★

The World Reagan Faces

NEARLY TWO AND A HALF years after Reagan had entered the White House, a longtime friend and occasional visitor, Billy Graham, assessing the condition of the world, declared that "judgment is coming."

Speaking as a spiritual leader, one doing his utmost to get people to see their condition in relation to God and to do something about it, the evangelist went on: "It seems that all the signs are pointing to Armageddon. The storm clouds are gathering, the lightning is flashing, the thunder is roaring. The great Armageddon could be now or a hundred years from now. We don't know."[1]

But he noted how often words like Armageddon were being used in religious and secular circles alike in our day. They seemed to hold a fascination for writers of all kinds. Armageddon—the Apocalypse—the end of the world. People, as they so often are in beholding that which terrifies them, can't take their eyes, or their minds, off the thought. They become transfixed. Their pulses race, they babble on. But they do little.

Graham spoke of the similarity between the road to Armageddon and the road to the Old Testament destruction of Sodom. He pointed out that Jesus indicated the problems of Sodom would be repeated as the signs of the times before His second coming. And, of course, many Bible believers say Armageddon will precede Christ's return.

Those problems, as described by the prophet Ezekiel, were pride, a surfeit of food, and prosperous ease and idleness. The people "were haughty and did abominable things" before God, Ezekiel summarized. Simultaneously they refused to aid the poor and the needy.[2]

For Graham, this fairly well described the condition of many people and nations today. "The people of Sodom were just too busy for God," he said, "too busy with their pleasures, too busy with making money to take any time for God." They had other idols—pleasure, money, sex, food, drink. The parallel does seem accurate.

Could it be the barest trace of guilt—an indelible sense—that causes us to dwell frequently upon the subject of Armageddon? Are we indeed racing toward it?

If so, what does this spell for our governmental leaders?

There are other, more secular observations than Graham's, of course, although they may be rooted in the same basic conditions, but bearing different names. The conflict of nations, for instance, causes us to think not in terms of individual sin but of the haves and the have-nots, the developed and the underdeveloped, the Western World and the Third World. And there is communism versus capitalism, totalitarianism versus democracy, white versus nonwhite.

All the conflicts, however, can be traced to the same event: man's rebellion against God's sovereignty, known in religious language as The Fall. Man refused to accept the terms in God's kingdom and chose to set up his own, with himself as the sovereign. The upshot was the proliferation of individual, man-governed kingdoms to a level of billions. And they all rival not only God's kingdom, but also one another. They are scrambling for dominance and influence over one another. I become the lord of my kingdom, you become the lord of yours. We set our own rules and our own goals. And we try to extend our influence over each other in our desire to become lord of as much as possible.

Complicating the process, adding meanness and ugliness to it in geometrically multiplied proportions, are the two underlying traits that entered the world at the time of The Fall—pride, which set the whole thing off, and fear. First, the fear was fear of God, but that led to fear of other men. From there—from pride plus fear—have sprung the evils besetting mankind throughout history.

At the same time the conflict of the ages has been waged at a cosmic level that exceeds the human's ability to think about it but yet touches him. That is the struggle between good and evil, between God and his adversary, Satan. It is not a contest between equals, for God the creator has no equal. Satan is a created being—perverted, corrupted from his original beauty—but nonetheless created by the Creator, who is the only truly free being in the universe.

Their conflict, whose outcome was decided before it began, was set in motion when God made it known (as revealed in Genesis 3:15) that He would overcome the results of The Fall and restore the one true kingdom—His. The billions of rival kingdoms will come down. But the conflict still rages, intensifying, taking many shapes periodically according to nations, empires, hemispheres, or individual criminal minds.

Therefore, Graham's view is an accurate one. But so are those that utilize terms like world hunger, nuclear holocaust, racial hatred, economic chaos. They are, at root, manifestations of the same conflict.

Pat Robertson, the television executive, described it this way: "The world has reached the stage where disaster looms on every hand. Everything seems to be going wrong, and the forecast is worse."

He pointed to the economy, defense, energy, crime, poverty, morality, education, hunger, and pollution. Each area, he said, carries the same theme—hopelessness.

"We cry out for solutions to problems too big for us," he lamented. "Our governments are on the verge of collapse; our finance is chaotic, our atmosphere polluted, our populations so massive that millions starve. Fear reigns."[3]

Where there is fear, there is greed and disease and war—and deeper fear.

One of the most encouraging and stimulating notes sounded from the economic sector in years gives us hope in coping with such a pessimistic outlook. It comes from George Gilder, the scholar and author who fortunately at one point had a good reading among key figures in the Reagan Administration, especially with his book *Wealth and Poverty.* As you read his ongoing work, you are struck with the conviction that we need not succumb to our problems—poverty, disease, pollution, hatred, war, and the like. Using different words, he convinces you that Robertson, in *The Secret Kingdom,* was on the mark in arguing that it is possible to live in such a manner as to overcome shortages, deprivation, poverty, and meanness. Robertson calls for living out, as individuals and as nations, the laws or principles of the kingdom of God and thus experiencing now that condition in which there is no diminishing of resources, but rather abundance.

Gilder, who speaks of faith in God somewhat more mutedly than Robertson, argues a strong case for free enterprise—capitalism—and drives at the same point of using to the fullest that which has been given to us by the Lord, maximizing creativity, generosity, and free-dom.

Neither he nor Robertson wants or expects to thwart God's purpose. The rival kingdoms—world systems—alien to God's purpose will come down. There will be difficulty. But faith in God and faith in the future will bring forth survival and with abundance. In *The Wealth of Families,* published by the American Family Institute in Washington, Gilder said that "by a narrow, rational calculus, the human predicament is always impossible." He went on:

"The great problem in contemporary society is that this narrow, rational calculus prevails and thus leads to a kind of despair. This in turn leads to programs of planning and control that exclude precisely those surprises of human creativity that have always overcome all our human difficulties. . . .

"The essential point is that experts [those utilizing the narrow, rational calculus] are always wrong on these major issues affecting future policy. And to the extent that we depend on experts and allow decision-making power to depart from families and individuals and businesses and churches and rise toward governments, the human creativity that is indispensable to overcoming our problems is thwarted, and the very horizons of the future are beclouded."[4]

The problem encountered by the ideas of Gilder and Robertson, and indeed by Reagan himself to some degree, lies within the "narrow, rational calculus" cited by Gilder. Graham noted it in his references to the people as being too busy for God. The opinion-makers of our day—those forming what might be called "the political nation"—to a large degree have totally ignored God as they attempt to influence and steer society through the minefield stretched before it. "Ignored" is probably too generous a word in most cases; "rejected" is more accurate. Many actively oppose any attempt to bring our considerations into harmony with the purposes of God. And we must hasten to point out that this opposition began in most cases with the best of intentions. There was genuine fear of religious or creedal oppression, based on ugly mistakes of the past. But that fear produced the same result it did in the Garden of Eden: a rejection of God's authority and ultimately a rejection of Him. Disaster follows.

It's unfair to isolate news people for criticism in this matter. Big business, labor, academia, the bureaucracy, authors—all share the responsibility. But journalists are the easiest to talk about.

There are exceptions, obviously, but news people generally are committed, almost with a blood oath, to what their profession has come to regard as "objectivity." This is taken so seriously as to create an amorality—a suspicion not only of anything that is bad but also of anything that is good. The results of this are slow to accumulate, but they do mount up. For when one is dealing with God, to reject or to ignore Him does not stop there. An almost imperceptible hardening accompanies it. Over a period of time the hardening piles up, like calluses. It becomes more and more difficult to perceive the goodness of God and His ways.

Further, because of the nature of mankind and particularly of those devoted to journalism, a news person cannot stand still in his increasing blindness to the reality of God, so he substitutes standards developed by him and others like him. He makes his judgments based on knowledge, insight, and prejudices from which he has totally excluded God. He has removed God from the equation.

The tragedy is that news people—and all who fall into such a trap—truly do not believe they have wandered from their objectivity. They do not see that they have wandered into a religion called humanism that worships man as God and have abandoned their objectivity. Another sad part is that, at least until fairly recent times, those who had taken such a course far outstripped their opposites in the development of the natural skills, talents, and drive necessary to report on the rapidly changing world. Those who persisted with a godly world view lagged so far behind in journalistic ability and concern for the world as to be unreliable.

I remember sadly the many discussions I held on these matters with news people who ranked with the best in the world. The genuineness of their commitment to uncommitment—a sort of vulnerable sterility—was unchallengable.

One of Washington's leading news executives, a friend, made it plain in a quiet, foot-on-the-desk conversation one hot spring morning in the mid-seventies that he believed a commitment to Christ would destroy the impartiality and objectivity required to function as a responsible newsman. He indicated no intention to bar such people from his staff, but it was clear he would not hold them in as high regard as he would atheists or agnostics.

Such discussions, and others in major news centers, provoked a probing assessment of such ideas as Christ's being "the truth" or of God's being completely free. What was one to make of the thought that Christ, who loved everyone enough to die for everyone, really had no axes to grind? Is He or is He not impartial?

So the problem is clear. News people, on whom our society, our government, our business have become dependent, employ a "narrow, rational calculus" in the name of objectivity to influence us powerfully in our decision-making. They are not evil. They are not conspirators. They are simply in error. But so are the other segments of the political nation. They perform their powerful functions by studying shadows, not full-blown reality.

It must be said clearly: They are not to be cursed. They are to be legitimately outperformed by those who have not removed God from the equation or fallen into the use of the narrow, rational calculus. We will deal with this in more detail in a later chapter.

So goes the world—and thus the United States.

It's the situation faced by Ronald Reagan. Jimmy Carter faced it. Gerald Ford faced it.

The symptoms have been written about ad nauseam from every angle—the economy, defense, centralized government, abortion, prayer, crime, urban deterioration, farm failure. Every conceivable solution has been prescribed. Some have been tried. Few have worked.

As for Reagan, he, the man who from all indications has placed his faith in God, has had some successes in battling the trends. After midterm, the economy did begin to improve. At the three-quarter mark, even unemployment was modifying. Three consecutive yearly income tax cuts seemed to be good medicine despite the skeptics. Industrial production was up. Housing starts rose. Budget-balancing was coming much harder, though, as interest on national debt climbed above the hundred-billion-dollar level to give defense and entitlement programs a run for the money. It seemed clear to the average citizen that this must be attacked, but the experts continued to look the other way, trying to get everything out of defense and domestic programs.

Many people winced in the last two years as Pat Robertson, by way of the "700 Club" TV program and his writings, called for consideration of some form of debt forgiveness in the manner of the Old Testament's Year of Jubilee. While such thoughts were being ignored or ridiculed, the cost of the debt continued to plunge this country, and others, toward financial collapse. It's worth noting that removal of that one item would thrust our country within shouting distance of a balanced budget.

Meanwhile, Reagan's New Federalism was struggling. His environmental record was under fire, especially in regard to James Watt, the former Secretary of the Interior. Defense issues also bubbled furiously, as sincere people waffled between a desire to restore international security and a desire to reduce high military spending. The burgeoning peace movement also figured prominently in this struggle.

Internationally, Reagan was having his problems. Latin America was especially difficult for him, specifically El Salvador and Nicaragua. The issue simply was how much should the United States assist those struggling against Marxists or Communists. In El Salvador, the leftists were trying to overthrow the government; in Nicaragua, they were trying to stay in power.

Reagan's basic view was that the Communists aimed to take over the hemisphere and indeed the world and were thus to be resisted, hopefully without dragging the United States into a war. His opponents felt he magnified the Communist threat and ignored the oppression suffered in many Latin American countries.

It should be noted that underlying the Reagan view for many, including numerous Christians, was the conviction that the greatest expression of love for anyone facing Communist domination is to help him resist. The idea was that refusal to resist, a seemingly loving and humane stance on the surface, was actually cruel since it would lead to a spiritual tyranny worse than material tyranny. The forced practice of atheism, the denial of God and the teaching of such denial to children, was the ultimate cruelty to many. We will look at this more closely later.

The Middle East was also a pulsating problem for the Reagan Administration. The issues dominated the news—Lebanon and the foreigners on its soil; Israel and the Palestinians; Syria and its designs; Moscow's intentions in the wider oil-laden area; Muslims versus Jews versus Christians. Usually ignored was the significance of the region to God's purposes for the world in the past, the present, and the future.

Overall, despite the thorns at every turn, Reagan appeared at the three-quarter mark to have begun to turn things his way at least a bit. His staff, given to dissension and jealousies and stupid missteps just like every other staff, didn't always help him, despite a fierce individual loyalty on the part of those closest to him. But the conservatives were beginning to make a mark, at least in terms of tone and attitude. And some new policies were indeed working.

As usual, nationwide polls were not terribly useful in trying to assess the administration's impact across the land. Quite understandably, they ebbed and flowed readily according to the nightly news or the morning front page, and reliable trends were difficult to monitor. However, with the exception of those people hurt by unemployment—and that was a major exception—there seemed to be an increasing optimism in the land. There was some sense that things—governments, industries, homes—could be made to work. People seemed to feel society, although still corrupted, was not as out of control as it had been.

Unhappily, despite economic progress, other nations generally did not seem to reflect the same optimism as found among Americans. There were still far too many have-nots. And the prospects for solutions were not fully persuasive. However, America's stature had improved and its progress was increasingly visible, enhancing the outlook for desperately needed international leadership. Perhaps Reagan offered hope in this area after all, some mused independently.

Still, the world for the most part was in depression, if not physically then spiritually.

An hour of quiet, previously unreported dinner conversation as the administration approached the halfway mark probably provided the most candid description of progress to date. It was general, but sounded honest.

The moment occurred in Peoria, with entertainers. The House minority leader, Robert H. Michel of Illinois, was being sorely contested for re-election and even appeared headed for possible defeat. And, though Michel had on occasion opposed Reagan's positions, the president wanted to campaign for him.

Pat Boone's considerable campaign skills were also sought and he arrived at his hotel in Peoria in the late afternoon with barely enough time to make a sound check with his band, have a bite of supper, and change clothes.

"I got a call from White House security that the president would like me to join him for dinner," Boone recalled. "I had already ordered food and, explaining that to the security man, I said, 'Well, I'll come up and have a cup of coffee,' and I was just assuming there would be a whole flock of people there and it wouldn't matter if I ate or not."

So at 6:30 Boone was dressed and a White House man led him downstairs and then onto a special elevator that carried him upstairs to the Presidential Suite. "I went in," he said, "and was looking around for the crowd, and there was none. I went back into the dining area and there was Ronald Reagan and Charlton Heston, and another place was set for me.

"It was just three actors now, having dinner together, and we laughed and told stories. And we got onto telling about how we had been mistaken for other people at various times in our careers. And the president said, 'Yeah, I was in Japan once when I was governor, and one Japanese fellow said, "Ahhh, you my fav'rite actor. I love your movie *Bridge on River Kwai.*" And I said, "No, that was William Holden; I'm Ronald Reagan," and the fellow without hesitating said, "Ahhh, you the other one. You my other fav'rite!" ' "

Boone, reconstructing the event after some months, shook his head and chuckled. "But then we talked about political things and the way things were going and so forth. And he was genuinely proud of the gains that were being made at that point.

"It was tough going and there was lots of opposition, he said, and there was no acrimony or harshness in his voice. 'We're getting there,' he said, 'and we're really making a difference. I see the indicators, and they're good. Overseas there were questions—I was an unknown quantity to them; they had had pictures painted. But as I got the chance to meet some of these leaders, I can see that we can develop some rapport.'

"But mainly he was optimistic about the economy and the government. 'We're making a turnaround,' he said."

And Michel was re-elected, although the Republicans lost considerable ground in elections across the country, following American political tradition at midterm.

As we assess the U.S. and the world today, it is apparent that people yearn for the same things they always have. They want economic security, appreciation, and a healthy, long life.

Unfortunately, they have come to look for these things from government. And they haven't found them there. Even in health, in which government-sponsored work has sometimes led to medical discoveries or programs, the overall gain is slight if it exists at all. Disease is rampant, even though life spans have increased. One cure seems to be followed by two new problems.

Yet, the Bible says these three great desires of mankind are available—riches, honor, and life. Why haven't our leaders pointed the way?

"The reward for humility and fear of the Lord is riches and honor and life."[5]

It sounds so simple. And it is—simple, but with a price. The price, basically, is pride. It must go. There can be no fear or reverence of the Lord as long as pride blocks the way. A proud man will not fear the Lord. He will not place himself under the authority of God. A meek man will. Seeing his own weakness, he will place himself under God's strength, under God's authority and discipline. Then, according to the framer of the proverb, the door is opened for the provision of riches and honor and life, the fulfillment of man's yearnings. He will even inherit the earth.[6]

The saddest part of this is that the segment of society allegedly believing this truth, now and in past decades, has set a terrible example for the world. For the most part, Christians have not proved that this truth is true—this truth and many others proclaimed by Jesus. We have presented an impoverished caricature of the abundant life Christ said He came to provide.[7] It attracts few. We have not established ways to lead people out of the quagmire, to bless them, prosper them, stimulate them. We have not shown forth the bright, living colors of the kingdom of God, but rather the dull grays and dirty whites of half-life. In fact, we have missed God's point in calling a people to Himself, getting them straightened out, and then empowering them to serve. We often are just as guilty of ignoring God as those who reject Him outright. Yet the words have been plainly before us, in a book of the Bible that we especially cherish:

> Is not this the fast that I choose:
>   to loose the bonds of wickedness,
>   to undo the thongs of the yoke,
> to let the oppressed go free,
>   and to break every yoke?
> Is it not to share your bread with the
>   hungry,
>   and bring the homeless poor into your
>   house;
> when you see the naked, to cover him,
>   and not to hide yourself from your
>   own flesh?
> Then shall your light break forth like
>   the dawn,
>   and your healing shall spring up
>   speedily;
> your righteousness shall go before you,
>   the glory of the Lord shall be your
>   rear guard.[8]

Too often, the ones heeding these words have been those who ignored the simultaneous evangelistic message of the historic faith. They preached and tried to practice a social gospel but fell short because they forgot personal salvation. Ultimately, they produced what Jacques Ellul, the French social critic, considered to be a "false presence of the Kingdom."[9]

Most damagingly, those who have placed their faith in God have given the world very few clues about how He can transform minds and bodies, talents and gifts, to new levels of creativity and excellence. We accepted the gospel and its salvation message, but we fell short in living out the life set forth by Jesus. We overlooked the principles of the kingdom and eventually left the running of the world to those who chose to remove God from the equation. Yet Jesus said His followers were to be the light of the world.[10] They were to lead by serving.[11]

In short, we abdicated. We didn't learn how the world works. We didn't become excellent in all the disciplines. We were unable to compete with those who wanted to take the nation and the world in another direction.

But it's not too late. Nine in ten adults—88 percent—say they pray to God, according to a survey by George Gallup. And one in six reads the Bible daily, with one in three reading weekly or more often. Three in four declare that they would like to see religious beliefs "playing a greater role in people's lives," and nine in ten want more emphasis on traditional family ties and more respect for authority.

A redirection is possible. And we must not be deluded into thinking that it can only occur through numbers and ballot boxes. They are important when placed in the proper perspective, but the power to change does not lie ultimately in the popular vote. Power to change originates with God; there really is no authority except from Him.[12]

That being the case, we have this hope:

> If my people who are called by my name humble themselves, and pray and seek my face, and turn from their wicked ways, then I will hear from heaven, and will forgive their sin and heal their land.[13]

Those are the conditions Reagan—man of faith, man of conservative principle—faces as we lurch onward, through the eighties. They are the conditions any leader faces. Chaotic, threatening, hard times on the one hand; hope on the other. What will be our reaction?

Reagan, as we saw, is fond of a Benjamin Franklin quotation that provides one answer:

> He who shall introduce into public affairs the principles of primitive Christianity will change the face of the world.[14]

Pursuing the Reagan mystery, we will examine the prospects and perils of such advice.

★ ★ ★ ★ ★ ★ ★ ★ ★ ★ ★ ★ ★ ★ *7* ★ ★ ★ ★ ★ ★ ★ ★ ★ ★ ★ ★ ★ ★

A Willingness

IT WAS GOOD FRIDAY, 1981, two and a half weeks after an assassin's bullet came close to killing Ronald Reagan. The Roman Catholic Archbishop of New York, the late Terence Cardinal Cooke, looked into the sparkling eyes of the seventy-year-old convalescing president and said gently, "The hand of God was upon you."

Reagan grew very serious. "I know."

He paused for just a fraction of a second, then added, "And whatever time He's left for me is His."

To a listening world, it was a "nice," touching thing to hear and we quickly moved on to something else.

Although it's impossible for us to accomplish, it might be good to try to see this from God's point of view. We have to rely mainly on Holy Scripture to do it, but from those ancient writings, tracing their entire flow, we begin to see something of the magnitude of the exchange between Cooke and Reagan. The president, pace-setter for the Western World, was saying, in effect, "I have committed myself to doing God's will henceforth." As we saw in chapter 3, he has for some time had a sense of the divine will, but his words to the cardinal indicated a commitment and dedication to that will without reservation.

From an eternal point of view, which is hard for us to assume in our finite condition, the pain and the fear and the awful suffering of others felled that day may have been worth it to bring the President of the United States to the place where he would make such a public declaration. The world could be changed, as Ben Franklin suggested.

Monday, March 30, of that year began as a routine day for the president. It was his seventieth day in office. Rain fell, but the temperatures were moderate.

As many writers have noted, Reagan made at least two remarks that by nightfall had taken on prophetic proportions. First, in a sort of pep rally for 140 people holding sub-Cabinet jobs in the administration, he broke out one of his Thomas Paine quotations: "We have it in our power to begin the world over again."

Second, in the afternoon he went to the Washington Hilton to talk about economic progress before three thousand five hundred representatives of the AFL-CIO's building and construction trades department. The responses were lukewarm, but before long the following sentence was recalled by many: "Violent crime has surged 10 percent, making neighborhood streets unsafe and families fearful in their homes."

As he walked from the Hilton to the waiting presidential limousine minutes later, he was shot by John W. Hinckley, Jr., the son, ironically, of Christian parents. Three of the six bullets fired in a two-second span seriously wounded the Presidential Press Secretary, James Brady; a Secret Service agent, Timothy J. McCarthy; and a Washington policeman, Thomas K. Delahanty. A fourth glanced freakishly off the limousine, passed between the door and body of the car, and struck Reagan under his uplifted left arm. The slug came to rest an inch from his heart, missing the aorta by a whisker.

The scene played over and over on the nation's television screens as the population passed through another period of collective horror. How can this be? we agonized. John Kennedy. Martin Luther King. Bobby Kennedy. Would Reagan be added to the list? George Wallace very nearly had.

Before the year was out, two other world leaders would be shot by assassins. First, the pope was wounded in Rome on May 13, barely six weeks after the attack on Reagan. Then President Anwar Sadat of Egypt was killed in Cairo on October 6.

Reagan—who had been the target of an attempted firebombing at the governor's residence in 1968 and had toughed out several ugly confrontations with student mobs in the late sixties—survived again. And a lot of people agreed with Cardinal Cooke.

A significant action received relatively scant attention in the press, although to many it was the most important step taken in the wild hours of crisis. It came when Mrs. Reagan, who had barely arrived at the George Washington University Hospital, was being questioned by a television reporter. Confusion reigned. Jim Brady, who had been shot through the brain, was reported dead, then alive, then probably dying. The president, who was at first thought to have escaped the bullets, was said to be in good shape, but was soon found to be in trouble. No one knew anything about the assassin and his motives.

Mrs. Reagan, shaken but apparently in control of herself, told the reporter that she was going to go into the hospital chapel and pray. She asked the nation to pray with her.

She did as she said, and lots of people responded.

It was a "nice" touch, even for those little acquainted with prayer, but there was little, if any, reporting about the profundity of what actually took place:

Ordinary people touched the greatest power that exists—the source of all power—God Himself, the Creator of everything there is.

The president recovered speedily.

Brady, who had not been expected to live, survived in what his doctor called a miracle.

McCarthy and Delahanty recovered.

The government held steady.

The American people found some momentary unity.

Historians, however, will have to search hard in the accounts of those days to know that anything as powerful as rallying a people to prayer occurred.

It's a puzzle. But the truth is, the people responsible for such reporting simply don't understand. As we've noted, Paul said it best: "The unspiritual man does not receive the gifts of the Spirit of God, for they are folly to him, and he is not able to understand them *because they are spiritually discerned.*"[1]

Billy Graham understood. He went immediately to Washington.

So did Donn Moomaw, Reagan's California pastor. He was in Bermuda vacationing with his wife, but flew into the capital as soon as he received the word. The president, seeing him for the first time, blurted out, "What are you doing here?"

Moomaw was startled, but knew his man. "What do you mean asking—you just got shot!"

"Well, you shouldn't have come away from your vacation just for something like this," Reagan replied.

Moomaw merely shook his head, smiling.

Pat and Shirley Boone understood, too. Landing in Honolulu, they received word about the shooting and immediately were taken into a small side room to wait for another plane. "We were alone in there," Shirley recalled, "and we really began to war in the Spirit. I'm sure there were believers anointed by God to pray for those men who were injured, and you felt that, over and over again, a move of the Holy Spirit, leading you, using you to pray and intercede for those men."

"And we knew he [Reagan] was going to be all right," Pat interjected, "and not like in the Kennedy situations where reports just got worse and worse."

Executives of the Christian Broadcasting Network understood. They put out word immediately that update news breaks on the cable network were to conclude with a call by the network president for the nation to pray for the recovery of Reagan and the others.

Yes, many people, big and small, understood.

For many Americans, the assassination attempt and aftermath provided their first deep insight into their president. They saw him in danger, fearful, hurting. And they liked what they saw. He kept them going—with a style they hadn't seen in a long time, if ever.

It began with a word to Nancy when she arrived at the hospital: "Honey, I forgot to duck." Reports of that quotable theft from Jack Dempsey in 1926 reassured an anxious nation. But it was only the first in a stream of verbal optimism that poured out of a frightened but undaunted man to lift the spirits of his people. Even as he entered the operating room and looked around at the surgeons poised to go to work on him, he quipped, "Please tell me you're all Republicans." Somehow, it was going to be all right.

After his operation, tubes in his throat threatened to interrupt the outbursts of wit, but Reagan merely turned to pencil and paper. After coming out of anesthesia in the recovery room, he was asked how he felt. Scribbling a bit weakly with the pencil, he replied, "All in all, I'd rather be in Philadelphia," unashamedly stealing again, this time from W. C. Fields.

When told that a nurse would spend the night in his recovery room, he wrote, "Does Nancy know?"

On the morning after his surgery, he greeted his aides, "Hi, fellas. I knew it would be too much to hope we could skip a staff meeting."

And to one who said he would be happy to know that the government was running normally in his absence, he asked, "What makes you think I'd be happy about that?"

Thus optimism prevailed. Lou Cannon, a tough reporter who is no stranger to heroism and tragedy, wrote warmly in his Reagan biography about this aspect of those days:

> President Reagan, wounded on March 30, 1981, after two months and ten days in office, did not die. He survived to show the nation the wit and grace that was on daily display before his friends and family. . . . One-liners were the way that Reagan dealt with the mysteries of life and death. He used them to soften up audiences and to entertain his aides and to bring smiles to the faces of those he loved. One-liners were Reagan's badge of courage when he was deeply frightened. He used them to wash away the fear, and White House spokesmen repeated them to the American public, knowing they would serve as reassuring signals to the country that the president was unimpaired. They were the best of signals, and Reagan kept sending them. . . . The nurses laughed, and the nation laughed with them. The one-liners were the testimony of the man. . . .
>
> The attempt on Reagan's life had, in fact, many results. In the short run it produced a wave of popular sympathy which assisted the passage of Reagan's economic legislation. In the middle distance it slowed Reagan's learning curve on foreign policy and encouraged his inclination to over-delegate And in the long run, Reagan's grace under pressure destroyed forever any lingering doubts that the president was a cardboard man whose aspirations and emotions were as synthetic as a celluloid screen. The heroism reflected in Reagan's humor was genuine, and everyone knew it. Forever afterward, criticisms of Reagan's policies would be separated from an evaluation of the man.[2]

Certainly, facing death made a deep impact on Ronald Reagan. Like all real-life tribulations, it turned theory into flesh-and-blood reality. Philosophy, religion—they either wither and blow away in the hardships of life, or they seep from the mind down into a man or woman's essence, that place the Holy Scriptures call the heart, the seat of being. There they truly become part of life.

I've often wondered what Christ's friend Lazarus would have said to anyone who wanted to philosophize about life after death. I can almost hear him saying, "Hey, man, don't talk theory with me. I've been there!" His philosophy had slipped from his brain into his heart.

What are we to think about Reagan's declaration to Cardinal Cooke that the rest of his life belonged to God, which implies that he wants to do the will of God for the rest of his life? Is that possible?

Many intelligent people believe it is presumptuous to speak of doing the will of God. It is true we should be careful how we speak of such matters. Nonetheless, as we saw in chapter 3, the Holy Scriptures make clear that it is possible to do the Lord's will, to fulfill one's purpose in the eyes of the Almighty. All that is actually required, at least to begin, is desire. And in this case that has been expressed.

From there, the possibilities are endless. Jesus Himself illustrated this in His incarnate life. He showed what it meant to live in the will of God, and thus the kingdom of God, always submitting to the authority of the Father, always seeking to find His will and to fulfill it, never attempting to persuade Him contrary to His will. He described the relationship this way: "My food is to do the will of him who sent me, and to accomplish his work."[3]

Most of us try to excuse ourselves by pointing out that Jesus, after all, was the Son of God—God Himself. It was easy for Him to do. Not so. Jesus was God, but He was also man, having taken on full humanity, with its temptations, limitations, and sufferings. In addition to coming to earth to reconcile God and man, he also came to reveal God the Father and to give us an example of how to live as humans here and now, with Him. He showed us how to do His will, explaining, "Thy kingdom come, Thy will be done, On earth as it is in heaven."[4] We were to live in His kingdom—now—by doing His will as Jesus did.

We also find clearcut examples in the Old Testament. Joshua, who led the children of Israel into the Promised Land, provides one. He was a mere man, like the rest of us, yet God penetrated His understanding with these words:

> Be strong and of good courage; for you shall cause this people to inherit the land which I swore to their fathers to give them. Only be strong and very courageous, being careful to do according to all the law which Moses my servant commanded you; turn not from it to the right hand or to the left, that you may have good success wherever you go. This book of the law shall not depart out of your mouth, but you shall meditate on it day and night, that you may be careful to do according to all that is written in it; for then you shall make your way prosperous, and then you shall have good success. Have I not commanded you? Be strong and of good courage; be not frightened, neither be dismayed; for the Lord your God is with you wherever you go.[5]

What wonderful words those are for any national leader! And they are presented as possible. The central requirement for Joshua was to do God's will—which, to that point, was found in the Mosaic Law, the externally expressed will of the Almighty. Joshua was to turn neither to the "right" nor the "left," which is probably a good instruction for a political leader in our day. Interestingly, *he* was to be strong and courageous; he had to make an act of the will to be so. God, who was to be with him, would guarantee that act of the will. Joshua would then succeed and be prosperous, inheriting the land. He and his people would have full, abundant life.

Terry Fullam, one of the leading Bible authorities in the Episcopal church, made a strong point about the difficulties that will be encountered when people ignore the Lord's purpose. "To go against the will of God can do nothing but diminish life,"[6] he declared, pointing to a portion of Psalms that reviews some of the rebellion of the people of Israel, in which they demanded something they knew to be contrary to God's will. "He [God] gave them their request," the psalmist says, "but sent leanness into their soul."[7]

That may explain why so many of us lead such impoverished lives. And such lives are contrary to God's deepest purpose, as revealed in Scripture, whether we are dealing with individuals or nations. He wants His people to have life, power, and authority, not meanness, ugliness, and poverty. Paul made it plain: "You have come to fullness of life in him, who is the head of all rule and authority."[8] The secret, he said, is to "live" in Christ, which is to do the will of the Father.

Furthermore, as Fullam explained in a wide-ranging discussion of the possibilities of doing God's will today, "God's voice, when acted upon, brings peace and rest inwardly."[9] If the people of the world today need anything, it's peace and rest.

Fullam, who is the rector of Saint Paul's Church in Darien, Connecticut, and leader of weekly Bible-teaching sessions in Washington, D.C. for many years, talked of his own experiences in learning about God's will:

> In order to discern the Lord's will about something, I say, "Lord, I don't want to do this unless you want me to. If you want me to do it, incline my heart; if you don't want me to do it, disincline my heart."
>
> Then I talk with my wife, my friends, *proven counselors* [italics added]. And, very importantly, *I use the brains God gave me.* I weigh alternatives. And little by little things begin to happen. I find a solid, reasonable desire that I can trust growing within me to go one or another direction. . . . I cannot think of a single time where I honestly sought the Lord to hear His will and trusted Him to

incline or disincline my heart, that I failed to come to a decision I believed was the right one. And always I ended up doing what I wanted to do. Do not misunderstand me. I did what I *wanted* to do, believing God had governed my heart. God is not out to trick us. He *wants* us to walk in unity and harmony with His Holy Spirit.[10]

Now, those are the possibilities to which Ronald Reagan appears to have opened himself. He seemingly has dedicated the rest of his days to the Lord. Can a national leader—a political man—follow through on that dedication?

Much of what we've discussed, although certainly not all, was addressed primarily to individuals. What about the national implications?

Joshua was concerned about a nation. And many other promises of the Old Testament were specifically for the nation of Israel. But many were universal or, at the least, were addressed to people of faith from other nations. Great numbers of people do not appear to be a problem for God. However, when those great numbers are sharply divided into political entities, can the promises be worked out?

The unfolding Reagan drama, which we will examine from several vantage points, may yield answers.

Renewed Conviction

IN HIS FIRST TWO YEARS as president, a number of Reagan's conservative supporters were disappointed by the administration's performance on social, moral, and international issues. They knew the president was concentrating his firepower on an economic turnaround. They agreed it was critical. But deep down they felt he and his people lacked commitment on matters like abortion and prayer in the schools. From the outside it was hard for them to appreciate the political give-and-take required to keep the government running and to buy time for gains later.

Compromise is difficult for a religious conservative, for example. He tends to view church history as one compromise after another from the time of Christ, resulting in the steady dilution of faith and power to a point of near-impotency. Of course, there is a good deal of justification for that view, at least regarding certain periods.

A political conservative has much the same problem. He sees truth and common sense eroding right out of sight. He, too, is often correct.

So it was with a great deal of relief that these supporters thought they detected the beginnings of a turnaround in early 1983, after the Reagan first term passed the halfway mark. He seemed once again to be hitting the issues head-on with consistency, rather than obliquely and occasionally.

For the conservative Christians, he was particularly impressive, primarily because two major evangelical events provided back-to-back platforms for him—genuine "bully pulpits" of the kind that Reagan even before he was elected promised to exploit.[1]

The first was before the National Religious Broadcasters on January

31 in Washington, after which numerous Christian leaders were heard to proclaim it the most forceful, forthright speech ever given by a president. The 4,200 people jammed into the ballroom of the Sheraton Washington Hotel loved it, rising to their feet time after time for long ovations. Many thought they had already gone to heaven when they heard him confide, "I'm accused of being simplistic at times with some of the problems that confront us. I've often wondered— within the covers of that single Book [the Bible] are all the answers to all the problems that face us today if we'd only look there."

Declaring his intention to sign a proclamation making 1983 the Year of the Bible, he said: "I hope Americans will read and study the Bible in 1983. It's my firm belief that the enduring values . . . presented in its pages have a great meaning for each of us and for our nation. The Bible can touch our hearts, order our minds, refresh our souls."

Could this be the political leader of the country? He was declaring that Holy Scriptures could be useful in guiding the nation. That was heresy to the humanists. And that group would be heard from, through the American Civil Liberties Union, regarding the Year of the Bible. But Reagan didn't falter that afternoon. "When Americans reach out for values of faith, family, and caring for the needy," he declared, "they're saying, 'We want the Word of God. We want to face the future with the Bible.' "

Looking back and ahead to the static set off by those who are troubled when the Bible, God, and government are mentioned in the same breath, Reagan said he was "shocked" when the First Amendment was used as a reason to "keep the traditional moral values away from policymaking."

"The First Amendment," he declared, "was not written to protect people and their laws from religious values. It was written to protect those values from government tyranny."

He was striking, of course, at the heart of an argument that has raged for decades over what the amendment means. It simply says: "Congress shall make no law respecting an establishment of religion or prohibiting the free exercise thereof." It appears to mean that Congress cannot by law force anyone to adhere to a religion, but it just as pointedly says Congress cannot by law prohibit anyone from practicing his religion. Does it in any way suggest religion cannot be a part of public life? Seemingly not.

Regardless, Reagan pressed his point all the way: "I've always believed that this blessed land was set apart in a special way, that some divine plan placed this great continent here between the two oceans to be found by people from every corner of the earth—people who had a special love for freedom and the courage to uproot themselves, leave their homeland and friends to come to a strange land. And when coming here, they created something new in all the history of mankind: a country where man is not beholden to government, government is beholden to man."

The religious broadcasters were on their feet cheering before the last phrase was completed. One or two couldn't help recalling the biblical account of Abraham, who was sent out by God to a strange new land, leaving the security of old friends and familiar surroundings to fulfill the Lord's purpose.

Then with a power that his supporters hadn't heard since his campaign days—or so they recalled—the president spelled out once more his long-held positions on issues that many Christians believe lie at least indirectly at the heart of our national and world difficulties:

—Prayer in the schools. "I happen to believe that one way to promote, indeed to preserve, those traditional values we share is by permitting our children to begin their days the same way the members of the United States Congress do—with prayer. . . . No one must be forced or pressured to take part in any religious exercise. But neither should the freest country on earth ever have permitted God to be expelled from the classroom." Deploring the Supreme Court ruling twenty-one years earlier that termed school prayer unconstitutional, as well as later supporting rulings, he promised not to give up his effort to pass a constitutional amendment reinstating voluntary school prayer. "I am determined to bring that amendment back again, and again, and again, and again until—" Applause blocked the sentence's conclusion.

—Tuition tax credits. "There are five million American children attending private schools today because of emphasis on religious values and educational standards. Their families, most of whom earn less than twenty-five thousand dollars a year, pay private tuition and they also pay their full share of taxes to fund the public schools. We think they're entitled to relief." And he pledged to continue the struggle to secure tuition tax credits for deserving families.

—Abortion. "There is another struggle we must wage to redress a great national wrong. We must go forward with unity of purpose and will." They sensed where he was heading. How forceful would he be? "Let us come together, Christians and Jews, let us pray together, march, lobby, and mobilize every force we have, so that we can end the tragic taking of unborn children's lives. Who among us can imagine the excruciating pain the unborn must feel as their lives are snuffed away?" Even the veteran broadcasters winced at the force of the description. It was almost too graphic. "And we know medically they do feel pain." He had rung the bell hard. But he pressed on. "I know that many well-intentioned, sincerely motivated people believe that government intervention violates a woman's right of choice. And they would be right if there were any proof that the unborn are not living human beings. . . . Doesn't the constitutional protection of life, liberty, and the pursuit of happiness extend to the unborn unless it can be proven beyond a shadow of a doubt that life does not exist in the unborn?" The applause answered the question.

—Drugs and disease. "Each year, government bureaucracies spend billions for problems related to drugs and alcoholism and disease. Has anyone stopped to consider that we might come closer to balancing the budget if all of us simply tried to live up to the Ten Commandments and the Golden Rule?"

—Religious freedom. Citing responsibility to help the oppressed in foreign lands, he noted that Voice of America transmissions of Christian and Jewish broadcasts were being expanded and improved. "Now, these broadcasts are not popular with governments of totalitarian powers. But make no mistake, we have a duty to broadcast. Alexander Herzen, the Russian writer, warned, 'To shrink from saying a word in defense of the oppressed is as bad as any crime.' Well, I pledge to you that America will stand up, speak out, and defend the values we share. To those who would crush religious freedom, our message is plain: 'You may jail your believers. You may close their churches, confiscate their Bibles, and harass their rabbis and priests, but you will never destroy the love of God and freedom that burns in their hearts. They will triumph over you.' "

Applause and cheers filled the huge hall. The only ones not applauding as Reagan wound down his rousing talk, certainly the most precisely and biblically Christian message delivered to the NRB by a national political leader in memory, were the half-dozen pool reporters covering for the national press. Their faces betrayed no emotion. Had they understood what had happened? Their reports, for the most part, indicated not. They perceived Reagan as essentially having hammed it up before a friendly crowd, telling them what they wanted to hear regardless of conviction or priority.

Five weeks later, when the president went to Florida to pound his themes in even stronger fashion, they got angry but they still didn't see what was happening. The National Association of Evangelicals, representing the conservative, Bible-oriented, evangelical churches in America, was the host group. He had wowed the folks in Washington, but he raised them to unprecedented levels of optimism in Orlando. If there had been any loose ends after the NRB speech, they were nailed down by the end of March 8. Some ruffled feathers began to flutter across the land.

At the Sheraton Twin Towers in Orlando, however, there was happiness. It began when Reagan reminded the one thousand evangelical leaders that "there are a great many God-fearing, dedicated, noble men and women in public life, present company included." And, he said, those public men and women need the help of Christians "to keep us ever mindful of the ideas and the principles that brought us into the public arena in the first place."

Then he touched the first heartstring. "The basis of those ideas and principles," he said, "is a commitment to freedom and personal liberty that, itself, is grounded in the much deeper realization that freedom prospers only where the blessings of God are avidly sought and humbly accepted."

He followed with a broad stroke: "The American experiment in democracy rests on this insight. . . . Only through your work and prayers and those of millions of others can we hope to survive this perilous century and keep alive this experiment in liberty, this last, best hope of man."

It was typical Reagan, but warm, seemingly sincere, friendly. And he was ready to push into deeper water.

> I want you to know that this administration is motivated by a political philosophy that sees the greatness of America in you, her people, and in your families, churches, neighborhoods, communities—the institutions that foster and nourish values like concern for others and respect for the rule of law under God.
>
> Now I don't have to tell you that this puts us in opposition to, or at least out of step with, a prevailing attitude of many who have turned to modern-day secularism, discarding the tried and time-tested values upon which our value system is based. No matter how well intentioned, their value system is radically different from that of most Americans. And while they proclaim that they are freeing us from superstitions of the past, they have taken upon themselves the job of superintending us by government rule and regulation. Sometimes their voices are louder than ours, but they are not yet a majority.

It was a telling point—"their value system is radically different from that of most Americans," but their loud voice gives them positions of power. Indeed, it may be the most telling point in current American history. Are we being "superintended" by minority voices? If so, why?

Most of the president's themes were those he had expounded before the NRB, but his language overall was more urgent. His arguments sounded as though they had been carefully written. For example: "Freedom prospers when religion is vibrant and the rule of law under God is acknowledged. When our founding fathers passed the First Amendment they sought to protect churches from government interference. They never intended to construct a wall of hostility between government and the concept of religious belief itself."

He was more than ever precise on abortion: "More than a decade ago, a Supreme Court decision literally wiped off the books of fifty states statutes protecting the rights of unborn children. Abortion-on-demand now takes the lives of up to one and a half million unborn children a year. Human life legislation ending this tragedy will someday pass the Congress and you and I must never rest until it does."

Then he stepped onto ground untrodden in Washington. Strangely, it was on this section that he was the most severely treated in papers and on TV screens across the land. One wonders why. It almost seems that blindness and irrationality set in, for he was misquoted, under-quoted, and reviled. Readers and viewers were presented with a tone and a conclusion that did not exist.

He laid essential groundwork for his concluding thesis with several sentences that were virtually ignored by his critics. Absolutely necessary for an understanding of his arguments were these words: "We know that living in this world means dealing with what philosophers would call the phenomenology of evil or, as theologians would put it, the doctrine of sin. There is sin and evil in the world and we are enjoined by Scripture and the Lord Jesus to oppose it with all our might."

Then, clearly and plainly, he said this: "Our nation, too, has a legacy of evil with which it must deal." He directly acknowledged the shortcomings—the sin—found in America's ongoing history, but noted the capacity of the nation to recognize and eventually rise above "the moral evils of our past."

He pointed specifically by way of example to "the long struggle of minority citizens for equal rights." He added this, again loudly and clearly: "We must never go back. There is no room for racism, anti-Semitism, or other forms of ethnic and racial hatred in this country."

He appealed to his audience to use its skills and its influence to combat "hate groups in our midst."

"The commandment given us," he said, "is clear and simple: 'Thou shalt love thy neighbour as thyself.' "[2]

Most of the above was ignored by reporters, especially the line about our nation's "legacy of evil," our problems with sin. Being thus ignored, it was unknown to millions across the land who thought they detected hypocrisy in some of the words that followed. For the president moved quickly into his concluding points.

He briefly recalled the first press conference of his presidency, where he answered one questioner by pointing out that, "as good Marxists-Leninists," Soviet leaders had publicly declared "that the only morality they recognize is that which will further their cause, which is world revolution." He reminded the evangelicals that he had been "quoting Lenin, [the Soviets'] guiding spirit, who said in 1920 that they repudiate all morality that proceeds from supernatural ideas—that is their name for religion—or ideas that are outside class conceptions." In other words, Reagan said, "morality is entirely subordinate to the interests of class war." On the other hand, he added, "everything is moral that is necessary for the annihilation of the old, exploiting social order and for uniting the proletariat." Quite simply, to the Soviet leaders, as indeed to all secular humanists, morality is what they determine it to be, not what God or anyone else says it is.

Reagan followed with two other lines that received scant attention outside the hall where he spoke. "This does not mean we should isolate ourselves and refuse to seek an understanding with them," he said. "I intend to do everything I can to persuade them of our peaceful intent."

However, he made plain that he was not willing to compromise principle to accomplish this. "We will never give away our freedom," he said. "We will never abandon our belief in God. And we will never stop searching for a genuine peace."

Over the years, "better Red than dead" and "better dead than Red" have been among the many inflammatory slogans that tend to obscure sincere arguments. Conservative and liberal causes have lots of them, unhappily. Reagan, as he wound down in Orlando, started to run head-on into "better dead than Red" and probably wasted his point on a number of critical listeners as they in effect tuned him out. That was unfortunate, but perhaps inevitable, for to those believing in God, those willing to look even deeper than patriotism, he made a logical point. Others were blinded by hostility and misunderstanding. They read a sort of chauvinistic super-patriotism into a sound, religious explanation.

Here is the controversial passage in its entirety, with italics added for emphasis:

> A number of years ago, I heard a young father, a very prominent young man in the entertainment world, addressing a tremendous gathering in California. It was during the time of the Cold War, and communism and our own way of life were very much on people's minds. And he was speaking to that subject. And suddenly I heard him saying, "I love my little girls more than anything. . . ." and I said to myself, "Oh, no, don't. You can't—Don't say that." But I had underestimated him. He went on: "I would rather see my little girls die now, *still believing in God,* than have them grow up under communism and one day die *no longer believing in God."*
>
> There were thousands of young people in that audience. They came to their feet with shouts of joy. They had instantly recognized the profound truth in what he had said *with regard to the physical and the soul and what was truly important.*
>
> Yes, *let us pray for the salvation* of all of those who live in that totalitarian darkness—pray that they will discover the joy of knowing God. But until they do, let us be aware that *while they preach the supremacy of the state, declare its omnipotence over individual man, and predict its eventual domination of all peoples on the earth*—they are the focus of evil in the modern world.

Certainly there must have been exceptions, but it seemed that all the respected and hard-working reporters, commentators, and analysts who took upon themselves the responsibility for explaining this story to the people missed the point and logic of this part of the speech. And this was the part that received the prominent coverage.

Some columnists were enraged by the president's reference to "totalitarian darkness" and particularly his use of the words "focus of evil in the modern world." Their problem would seem to have been three-fold:

First, they forgot his umbrella references to the worldwide problem of sin and America's legacy of evil "with which it must deal," which suggests it hasn't been fully dealt with.

Second, they ignored his qualifying clause that said the Soviets were the focus of evil *while* they preached supremacy of the state, declared its omnipotence over individual man, and predicted its eventual domination of all peoples.

Third, they lacked perception as to the seriousness of living and dying without faith in God.

There's little that can be said about the first two points. They were oversights or omissions, brought about by whatever reason. One hopes they were not intended to deceive, but rather resulted from carelessness or haste. They produced distortion and unfairness.

The third point deserves further thought, for it lies at the heart of much misunderstanding in the world today regarding communism. In a way, anti-Communists brought it on themselves with their zeal, their tendency toward sloganeering, and the harshness of their rhetoric. Of course, McCarthyism and its relatives were deplorable and left marks that will be with us for a long time.

These excesses together have blinded many well-meaning people to the dangers of Communism, Marxism, Castroism, Maoism or any of the offshoots, at least as viewed by people of faith. And this view is reasonable and logical when cleared of smoke.

To the believer, life and death without God are hell. Whatever else it may mean, hell specifically means that: separation from God. Nothing is worse. And anyone who forces or teaches people to live in such a manner as to cause them to lose their faith in God is an instrument of evil. For according to the Holy Scriptures, people "by grace" are "saved through faith."[3] Their salvation—in this life and after death—comes through faith.

Now Communism teaches and enforces the general practice of atheism, which rules out faith and thus salvation.

That was the point of the president's reference to the "young man in the entertainment world" with the daughters. That young man, who was Pat Boone, obviously did not want his daughters to die. But he knew that their death as girls of faith would result in their eternal life in the presence of God—the ultimate happiness. Were their educations and lives to be dictated by those who day in and day out forced into their minds the belief that there is no God and forbade all expression of faith, he feared they might "one day die no longer believing in God" despite his secret efforts to teach them otherwise.

To the believer, death is not the source of dread that it is to an unbeliever. It is not the end. There is real life after that. He exists for that hope. This life, while precious to the believer and worth living to the fullest, is not the be-all and end-all. Life (before and after death) with God is the be-all and end-all. Thus, the greatest expression of love on the part of a believer is to do anything he can to facilitate that experience in another person's life. The greatest expression of cruelty is to do anything that might impede it.

That is one reason why, as difficult as it may seem, many sound people are so opposed to any action to "liberate" a nation and let its population slide into Marxism and Communism. If given only the two options, they would allow them to suffer right-wing oppression, if it did not dictate atheism. The truth, of course, is that those are not the only options available, although options leading to democracy and free enterprise require great perseverance and endurance.

Reagan, in Orlando, grasped this, and the evangelicals present recognized it. They knew with him that "while America's military strength is important . . . the struggle now going on for the world will never be decided by bombs or rockets, by armies or military might.

"The real crisis we face today," he said, "is a spiritual one; at root, it is a test of moral will and faith."

Characteristically grasping each side of the podium and turning his gaze from the right to the left and then back, he concluded, "I believe we shall rise to the challenge. . . . I believe this because the source of our strength in the quest for human freedom is not material but spiritual. . . . For in the words of Isaiah: 'He giveth power to the faint; and to them that have no might he increaseth strength. But they that wait upon the Lord shall renew their strength; they shall mount up with wings as eagles; they shall run, and not be weary.' "[4]

They were unusual speeches, both Washington and Orlando. Not exactly turning points, since the material was not actually new to Reagan's thinking, they were certainly milestones, a breakthrough of convictions, mounted with rare force and urgency.

The fallout was amazing. Hugh Sidey, *Time* magazine's customarily cool and reasonable observer of the presidency, abandoned his restraint in a column headlined "The Right Rev. Ronald Reagan." He was amazingly upset, even furious, but cynically clever.

"The Right Rev. Ronald Reagan journeyed last week to the holy precincts of the 41st annual convention of the National Association of Evangelicals in Orlando, Fla.," he wrote. "His fiery sermon mixed statecraft and religion. He made politicians from Moscow to Washington sore and brought the divinity-school crowd out of their paneled studies with flutters and shrieks."

Invoking touches like "sawdust trail," "brimstone," and "sulfurous blast," he bordered on poor taste when he spoke of Reagan's audience beginning "to see a halo glow faintly over his head and hear the rustle of feathers above," presumably referring to angels. But he was just warming up: Reagan "warned against 'modern-day secularism' and marched holier than thou into the forbidding swamps of abortion and teen-age sex. Reagan's righteous arm held high the Declaration of Independence . . . feathers were smoldering, eyes were moist, a first strike of prayers soared toward the Kremlin."

Having spent the sarcasm, he then concluded with frightening seriousness: "How we deal with the Soviets is not something that can be decided by self-anointed soldiers of God armed with unbending judgments about who and what are good and moral."[5]

Another brilliant writer, Anthony Lewis of *The New York Times,* screamed even more shrilly than usual, somehow reading into Reagan's words the implication that the president was denouncing as ungodly all those who favor a freeze on nuclear arms. And he, like Sidey, suggested inaccurately that Reagan declared Americans to be blameless in the world.

And so it went, across the country. Unfortunately, many people without access to the text of Reagan's speech depended upon such commentary for insight and, even those holding theological views similar to Reagan's were angered by what they *thought* he had said. Some even attributed statements to him that had not been made.

The president did not slack off. He had turned the corner into the final months of a first term and his convictions showed increasingly.

Principles were stated unequivocally even in the face of setbacks on school prayer in Congress and abortion in the courts. He had said he would fight on, and he appeared to be doing so.

His goals with the persistent tactics remained the same: one, a constitutional amendment that would allow voluntary individual or group prayer in public schools and other institutions while forbidding government officials to compose the words of the prayers; two, a law forbidding abortion except in cases of rape or incest and those where the life of the mother is specifically threatened.

But he didn't stop there. He called a National Day of Prayer, which received little attention in the general media and thus produced little action except among those already committed to intercede for the nation. He proclaimed 1983, as indicated, the Year of the Bible, despite a challenge led by the ACLU over the constitutionality of such a proclamation. With new vigor he strode into the midst of school issues, pressing educators to put a "much greater emphasis on the basics," including improved standards, learning skills, and "basic values of parental involvement and parental control." He urged that teachers, who he said had been "fighting a lonely war," receive merit pay. "It wasn't teachers who created and condoned the drug culture, sexual license, and violence in our society," he told the eighty-seventh annual convention of the National Parent-Teacher Association. "It wasn't teachers who encouraged the banality of TV over the beauty of the written word."

Reagan also kept up the pressure on international matters, following the themes revived in the NRB and NAE speeches. For example, on July 19, in a White House program held in observance of Captive Nations Week, he firmly placed the United States on the side of countries caught in totalitarian oppression.

"Today," he said, "we speak to all in Eastern Europe who are separated from neighbors and loved ones by an ugly iron curtain, and to every person trapped in tyranny, whether in the Ukraine, Hungary, Czechoslovakia, Cuba, or Vietnam, we send our love and support and tell them they are not alone. Your struggle is our struggle. Your dream is our dream. And someday you, too, will be free."

Despite concerns even within his own administration that he often became too forthright in talking about the Soviet Union, Reagan waded into the peace issue: "Now some believe we must muffle our voices for the cause of peace. I disagree. Peace is made—or broken—with deeds, not words. No country has done more or will strive harder for peace than the United States. And I will personally embrace any meaningful action by the Soviet Union to help us create a more peaceful, safe, and secure world. . . . With every ounce of my being, I pray the day will come when nuclear weapons no longer exist anywhere on earth.

"And as long as I am president, we will work day in, day out to achieve mutual and verifiable reductions in strategic weapons."

In the face of additional explosions south of our borders, he declared with unusual boldness that, "for the first time in memory, we face real danger on our own borders." He added: "We must protect the safety and security of our people. We must not permit outsiders to threaten the United States. We must not permit dictators to ram communism down the throats of one Central American country after another."

"Let us resolve today," he concluded, "there must be no more captive nations in this hemisphere. With faith as our guide, we can muster the wisdom and will to protect the deepest treasures of the human spirit: the freedom to build a better life in our time, and the promise of life everlasting in His kingdom."

Oddly, it was with a group of news editors that Reagan offered the best explanation of his burst of aggressiveness on social, moral, and international issues. In a report on the wide-ranging session, the *New York Times* said this:

> Reagan, in an expansive interview that was revealing about his attitudes toward government and the presidency, rebutted conservative critics who feel he has been compromising too much on the principles that they believe got him elected.
> "I know it can look that way," he said, quickly adding: "I'm not retreating an inch."
> "There are some people," Reagan said, "who would have you so stand on principle that if you don't get all that you've asked for from the legislature, why you jump off the cliff with the flag flying."
> The president said that "a half a loaf is better than none" and that unyielding critics had "misread" his tactics in dealing with different factions. "I am very stubborn," he said. "I come back and ask for more the next time around."[6]

Yes, Reagan, the man from the West, is stubborn. And he was asking for more. Once again his conservative guns were blazing, but he seemed more in control than ever, at least in terms of the direction he wanted to take this brawling, sprawling, ever-changing nation. His convictions showed plainly, those that had taken root in the little Illinois towns of his childhood, out among the ordinary people who were working, sweating, and laughing to stay alive, all under the eyes of a generous, God-fearing mother who taught him how to pray. He was an old-fashioned man who believed that true principles never died, and he was pushing them hard.

And he was pushing them in an unusual place—the capital, also old-fashioned in many ways but new and rowdy in others. What indeed was happening in Washington?

★ ★ ★ ★ ★ ★ ★ ★ ★ ★ ★ ★ ★ ★ *9* ★ ★ ★ ★ ★ ★ ★ ★ ★ ★ ★ ★ ★ ★

The Washington Atmosphere

WASHINGTON IS A nervous city. Its people fret a lot; they're tense and anxious, hanging on every news report, every rumor. They scowl often; when they laugh, they're often too loud. Life is rather up and down.

Now those are the government people, especially the political people and those feeding off them, everyone from lobbyists to news types. The regular run of folks really aren't all that wound up, but they're the quiet ones, and that lets the noisier ones set the tone.

And it's an unusual tone.

Consider the fact that no composer sat down to his piano and worked out something like "I left my heart in Washington" or "Washington, Washington, it's my kinda town." Despite the Redskins, no one croons "Autumn in Washington."

True, the city contains people from all over the country and the world, but it is rather a narrow, self-centered town. Indeed, it is myopic, convinced that everything worth bothering about, everything representative of mankind, happens essentially within its own borders.

Every now and then outsiders come along bearing grandiose plans for change. Real Potomac people merely chuckle. They know nothing changes in Washington. If anyone's going to change, it will be the outsiders.

And that's the way it's usually gone. Washington works its magic on people from California, Michigan, and Georgia. And now there's a new set of Californians. Are things the same? Is the tone getting better?

As we'll see when we take a close look at the "political nation" or establishment, much *is* the same. As one of the new Californians noted, "There is a Washington establishment that is kind of the quintessence of the liberal establishment; it represents what is done and what isn't done. It is essentially liberal in its orientation, but it's more than liberal politically. It has to do with values about religion; it has to do with ethical and moral values, and so on. And there is this disdain for people who don't believe in cutting each other up, people who don't believe in using the media to advance their own position, who don't believe in engaging in the power politics of Washington. They think there's something wrong with these people."

That sounds a lot like ten years ago, or twenty, or fifty. But, in some ways, it's worse. The power politics is still power politics. Sometimes it's dirty and despicable; often it's merely "hardball" (Washington loves its clichés). But the moral and ethical erosion is amazing, as one highly placed Californian noted. "Let me give you an example just in the last few days," he said. "We had two Congressmen—one liberal and one conservative, a Democrat and a Republican—involved in sexual misconduct with pages. And the Congress *reprimanded* them! I mean, what could be worse? It's not two equal adults engaging in something, even though wrong, but here were adults in positions of tremendous power using people who were in essence working for them—young people. You can't tell me there's not undue influence in that situation. I mean, this was the most reprehensible conduct I can think of—and they only *reprimanded* them! I still haven't recovered."

He paused one second. "You have to think about forgiveness also, which you do, but at least it should not be made such a trivial thing. Here's a real abuse of trust."

Washington, like much of the country, tends to shrug its shoulders at such episodes, failing to perceive that deterioration in values eventually seeps into all aspects of public life, including the decision-making process, which touches hundreds of millions of lives.

A colleague of the Californian, making a different point, traced the effects of the moral deterioration on power politics, showing how persistent "establishment" thinking can before long affect even the conservative outsiders, who might have been utterly moral to begin with.

"There are people in this administration who are pro-abortion despite the president's position," he said. Then he touched on the reasons. "The problem with abortion is that, it's such—it is probably the most divisive issue of our time in terms of domestic politics. There's just no center ground here, and what they see in their west wing view of the world is that we are entering an age of women in the majority, and Ronald Reagan is weakest in women's issues. And—to some of them—it makes absolutely no sense for him to go out and pound the drums against abortion. He is only digging himself in deeper and deeper. So there is this tremendous—there's a certain reluctance—on the part of some."

He had put his finger on the significance of a city's or a nation's atmosphere where government and politics are concerned. He had laid bare the truth about the importance of personal and collective morality among political leaders—once regarded as an inappropriate subject for public discussion. Loss of moral fiber produces a willingness to compromise principle, to crumble under political pressure.

In the case of abortion, for example—and there are other issues like it—moral deterioration creates a willingness to follow the relatively easy course established by a number of politicians in the last few decades. It consists essentially of deflecting decisions to the courts rather than facing up to them oneself. The courts are accountable to no one. Politicians have to go home and face the voters. So why not abdicate leadership and responsibility and succumb to the judiciary's willingness to legislate in the face of a vacuum?

Thus, re-election overtakes principle as the foremost consideration when moral fiber weakens. Ordinary citizens may get frustrated, the politician thinks, but they always get over it.

With that in mind, we should look at the Washington atmosphere with a spiritual perspective, since these are spiritual matters at root.

We should take note of the fact that well in excess of three thousand Christian groups, including churches, minister to the metropolitan Washington area. One leader estimated that two billion dollars a year are spent "to keep all the religious activities open."

In addition, Washington, as the capital of the world's most prosperous country, attracts Christian leaders from all parts of the globe to preach, teach, and otherwise bring their influence to bear. It receives more ministry than most cities of the world.

Yet Washington suffers as all cities do—with crime, drug, racial, poverty, and housing problems. Murders occur in the streets virtually every night. Rape is rampant. Divorce is commonplace. Old people suffer. Children are abused. Licentiousness runs full spectrum.

Why? There are many partial answers. But there is strong evidence pointing especially to two causes.

First, politics—in terms of strife, jealousy, envy, pride, and competition—is nearly as rampant in many Christian circles, especially among leadership, as in secular ones.

Second, much of the Christianity has become cultural and social rather than spiritual. As one of the city's most respected ministers put it, "The problem is that what we are preaching really is not Christ, the person, but Christianity, the system."

If you examine the two causes, you actually find one problem: Washington, like so much of America, has produced many, many churchgoers, but far fewer followers of Christ. And mere churchgoing will not, in the long term, produce people capable of withstanding the pressures of Washington or any other city. Just as we noted above in looking at moral deterioration and its effects on political life, seepage will occur. The church won't overcome the problems; the problems will overcome the church, all the way down to the power problems, the money problems, the sex problems, everything.

Experts describe all of this as a condition of carnal, not spiritual Christianity. Its proponents have not "crucified" the old, sinful nature nor taken on the nature of Christ. They have not been building the church that Jesus said would stand against all the powers of hell.[1]

As a result, there is considerable hypocrisy and it does not go undetected. The senator who campaigns on family issues and attacks pornography, adultery, and the like is known to be sleeping with his secretary. Two evangelists, nationally known for their work in leading hundreds to Christ, are both recently divorced and known to be sleeping with their secretaries.

Young people in the capital learn of this conduct and steadfastly refuse to have anything to do with church, preferring rebellion and dissipation.

Less obvious but still very real is the legislator, one of the four or five most powerful men in the capital, who day in and day out rushes from his committee hearings to lock himself in his office and spend half the day weeping over his family problems.

Another leader resigns from his powerful job, ostensibly for business reasons, but close friends know it is caused by a deteriorating family situation.

One Christian authority reported that 70 percent of the married members of the House and Senate were in marital difficulty of one degree or another. This is the area of life taking the worst pounding in Washington. Congressmen, for example, are forced to spend weekends campaigning and meeting with people in their home states, separated from their families, exposed to extraordinary adulation and temptation. Their wives can't handle the separation.

It's also well known, but little discussed, that financial problems ravage young congressmen and others today. They can't meet obligations and maintain appearances on their salaries, and they're afraid to vote for an increase. So they suffer, and skimp. Some sleep in their offices. Some eat poorly. Some with sizable families are helped by Christians simply to survive. Family problems are almost inevitable.

"It's a cesspool," lamented one well-known Christian activist. "A lot of times, just visiting the various places and seeing what's happening, I feel like taking a shower when I come home, to clean off."

Perhaps the saddest aspect of the condition is found among the elected and appointed people who go to Washington determined to serve the Lord. They're committed to Him. They intend to live righteously. But in three months, many of them are glassy-eyed, overwhelmed, trapped by the system. Those who survive in their close walks with the Lord are those with powerful interior discipline who refuse to abandon their prayer lives and their study of the Scriptures. Usually they have equally committed spouses and close Christian friends. The first thing they think of in the mornings is Christ. They seek His kingdom first and allow other things to follow.

Sadly, survivors like this are in the minority. But they do exist, and there's reason for optimism despite the woefully depressing horror stories. And the main reason for the optimism is the fact that, according to Christians who have worked in and around the halls of power for many years, political and governmental figures are the most open and receptive to the gospel ministry of any segment of society. "They are needy," one of the Christians said, "and they *know* they're needy. I can count on one hand the number of negative responses I've had in efforts to talk about the Lord on a personal basis." The last phrase is significant. These people, at least at first, are not interested in church or meetings. But they *do* want to talk about God and themselves. They want help. And they will respond to the Lord Himself in one-on-one situations.

Happily, more one-on-one situations, or at least small group situations, are occurring—reportedly more now than at any other time in history.

A wide range of ministries and individuals is responsible for the brightening picture, from single churches to multi-faceted organizations like Campus Crusade, Young Life, Inter-Varsity, and the Salvation Army. Critically important to the momentum are Christians within the government ranks who witness, pray, and conduct Bible studies from the highest to the lowest offices. Weekly Bible studies, running from a half-hour to an hour or more, sometimes in early morning, sometimes at noon, sometimes in the early evening, are found in every building, from the old executive office building to the Pentagon across the Potomac. Generals, clerks, senators, secretaries, department heads, White House aides—all kinds are involved.

These are the people who are going beyond what some call "easy believism" or the "cheap grace" of which Bonhoeffer wrote. They are the ones attempting to move from a mere Christian culture to the reality of following Jesus. They know a half-hour or forty-five minutes a week in deep fellowship are not enough; they need several hours a day, even all day. But they are at least striving to move in the right direction.

Jesus said, "Follow me," and the disciples left their jobs and followed Him.[2] Twentieth century man seems unable to bring himself to that kind of obedience. But more and more are trying.

Jesus also said, "If any man would come after me, let him deny himself and take up his cross *daily* and follow me."[3] It was to be a total, daily commitment. "For whoever is ashamed of me and of my words, of him will the Son of man be ashamed when he comes in his glory and the glory of the Father and of the holy angels."[4] Privacy was not to be carried too far. Faith was personal, yes; private, no.

Those were the sort of things being grappled with in the small meetings. What do they mean for modern man? A Washingtonian? A politician?

It was very hard for any serious-minded Christian. He knew the answers. But the execution was painful. It produced the kind of "suffering" of which the New Testament writers warned. It was outright tribulation in many cases—even persecution.

Dee Jepsen spoke of the Washington atmosphere in terms of the witness of the broader Christian community. "I think there is a change," she said. "There is much more openness about it in my view—about Christian commitment—by more people. We have a lot more evangelical outreach dinners, luncheons, that sort of thing, going on, Bible studies being organized, and a lot more upfront Christian activities."

She recalled particularly a black-tie event at the Kennedy Center quite early in the Reagan administration that was sponsored by the American Christian Heritage Foundation, on which she serves as a board member. It featured Carol Lawrence, in the premiere performance of "Mary, Mother of God," and also Pat Boone.

"The *Washington Post* absolutely could not figure out what was going on," she chuckled. "We had to turn away hundreds—twelve hundred—as I recall. And the *Post* really couldn't understand it. They kept calling people with some sort of involvement and saying, 'Now this isn't a fund-raising thing; so why are you doing it?' In fact, there was no charge. And Nancy Reagan was the honorary hostess, and there were a lot of people from the White House there. And the paper just could not believe that someone would spend money and have a big gathering like that without some ulterior motive. And what we said was that there just were a number of us who live and work in this city, as many other thousands do, where there are problems that seem to be without solutions, and we need some strength beyond ourselves and some answers beyond ourselves, and we find those answers and that strength in a relationship with Jesus Christ. And we just want to share that joy."

The senator's wife reflected a moment. "They did write an article," she went on, "and it was accurate—and I appreciate that very much. And they said something like, there was no honored guest last night at the big affair at the Kennedy Center, unless you call Jesus Christ the honored guest."

She smiled brightly. "Now, wasn't that neat?"

And it was not an isolated event. Christians have been increasingly visible. Following the Redskins' awesome triumphs in the 1982–83 professional football season, for example, an "outreach dinner" attracted upwards of five hundred people to hear the testimony of Coach Joe Gibbs. "They were the upper crust," Mrs. Jepsen said, "people that you don't always reach otherwise, who came if for no other reason than curiosity."

Robert Pittenger, a former leader in Campus Crusade, was the host at this sumptuous event and others like it that are held every few months. "They heard the gospel head-on," declared Mrs. Jepsen.

There were other kinds of witness, too, quiet, but profound, heart-warming to some, perplexing to some. One of the most exemplary, and surprising, occurred in the Cabinet Room at the White House.

Margaret Heckler, former Representative of Massachusetts, had been appointed Secretary of Health and Human Services (once the Department of Health, Education, and Welfare). Meeting with representatives of the pro-life movement, she spoke before the president arrived—her first such session since being appointed to the Cabinet post. As reconstructed by someone present, her remarks went this way:

> I want to tell you how pleased I am to be here today. I lost a very difficult campaign [for re-election to Congress] and now I'm appointed to this office. And I just want you to know that I feel the hand of God on my shoulder.
>
> Because of the nature of my belief and my philosophy of life and the person I was running against, there were many prayer groups praying for me around the state. I lost. But there was one Christian woman who told me that the Lord kept taking her to a passage in the Bible that she felt showed her I would be placed in a "council with the elders," and she said she hadn't thought I was going to win.
>
> I believe I have providentially come to this office, and I'm very grateful to the Lord, and I'm very grateful to this president.
>
> And I feel very strongly about the sanctity of human life, and I do not believe it is a coincidence that my first meeting is with a group of pro-life leaders.
>
> Now, I've not served in this office before. Maybe you're not supposed to talk like this. But this is the truth.

Mrs. Heckler, a Roman Catholic with two daughters involved in charismatic renewal, carried her expression of faith a step further in a later and smaller meeting of a Cabinet Council. She opened it with a prayer, a remarkable and perhaps precedent-setting step, at least in recent years.

The Cabinet is not without other serious-minded Christian representation, however. Meese, Counselor to the President and a member of the Cabinet, is a believer. Others who are vocal about their faith are William P. Clark, newly appointed Secretary of the Interior; Donald Hoedel, Secretary of Energy, and Elizabeth Dole, Secretary of Transportation. Several other Cabinet officers reveal at least a nominal commitment to the Lord, and most attend churches.

Wives of Cabinet members also meet weekly for Bible study and prayer with a representative of the Christian Embassy (Campus Crusade), and a number of them are quite mature in their Christian experience.

Among the military stationed in and around Washington are a high percentage of active Christians. At the Pentagon, Bible studies and prayer meetings are commonplace. And they begin right at the top, with General John W. Vessey, Jr., the chairman of the Joint Chiefs of Staff, who is refreshingly open in the expression of his faith. He meets regularly for prayer and Bible study with the other chiefs and on other occasions with men from civilian offices, including Meese and Ellingwood. Admiral James Watkins, Chief of Naval Operations, meets with others for similar purposes. In a workhorse speech entitled "The Moral Man," which he has delivered at several events around the country, he says in effect, "I'm here as the Chief of Naval Operations, but I'm also here as a Christian."

Despite the anguish found among many, as we noted, the story is much the same on Capitol Hill, although the percentage of openly professing believers is not high. The Senate prayer group, which has been functioning for about forty years, has spawned numerous smaller groups of two, three, and four people who meet periodically to pray, to hold one another up, to intercede for God's blessing on the nation. As one minister of the gospel related, "I could give every minute of every day just working with the response in the Senate and the House— just with individuals who want to go deeper with Christ."

Many of the professing Christians in the Senate are well known— Mark Hatfield, William Armstrong, Roger Jepsen, Gordon Humphrey, Sam Nunn, Lawton Chiles, Don Nickles, Pete Domenici, Strom Thurmond, Jesse Helms, Jeremiah Denton. Similarly, in the house are Mark Siljander, Marvin Leath, Carlos Moorhead, Jack Kemp, Bob McEwen, Don Bonker, Paul Trible, and Bill Whitehurst. And there are others.

Wives of senators and representatives also meet regularly for Bible study and prayer. And it is not insignificant that a number of believers are scattered about various areas of the Capitol property itself. Several women in the dining rooms show forth the love of God in remarkable ways, quick to smile, quick to speak a kind word, quick to talk about the Lord. Outside, policeman Bill Ashton can be seen helping people, talking about Christ, and sharing his joy in numerous ways. These various presences are obviously examples of the "salt of the earth" Jesus spoke about.[5] Such faithfulness has the potential to revolutionize the lives of the thousands who pass by.

In the judicial branch, a reading of Christian activity is more difficult to come by, in keeping with the nature of the legal process. Judges and their aides tend to be undemonstrative even when possessing a spiritual awareness. Among the Supreme Court justices, Sandra Day O'Connor has talked about her Christianity and values and Chief

Justice Burger is said by those in a position to know to be "open" to discussions about the Lord.

I talked to several in high Washington positions about the effects of their commitment to Jesus Christ upon their approach to their jobs. I was particularly struck by the sincerity and effectiveness of the head of one agency, which had passed through troublesome times in the early days of the administration and now appeared to be functioning well. He felt his direction should not be singled out for special merit but rather was merely indicative of "something others are also doing."

He described his approach briefly:

> I come in in the morning and I spend time here, before we do anything else, praying, reading the Bible. And I encourage all my department heads who are born again—and that's quite a few—to do the same. I encourage them—before they take the first telephone call, talk to their secretaries, take a message, pick up a piece of paper—to pray and spend some time in meditation in the word.
>
> And I go from office to office [before they arrive] praying in their rooms and over their typewriters—and I pray for, you know, I pray for all kinds of things here.

He quickly made it clear there was nothing coercive about his approach.

> There are a lot of things that it's not, and there are a lot of things it is. . . . I've prayed with almost everybody I've fired, for example. But it's not in the sense of coercion or an extra discipline or whatever. I've fired people who were Christians. [Some] were part of Bible studies that I happened to be in—we've had personal relationships. And I know that, regardless of why they're leaving here, God still has—they're part of God's family—and He still has a purpose for them. This is good in a sense, because it shows— hey, as a manager, it doesn't mean you have to keep everybody just because he's a Christian! On the other hand, it doesn't mean that you violate Christian principles by the way you fire them—or that you can't have a Christian relationship when they leave.

As this conversation was ending, the government official received a call from another agency director who wanted to talk about some decisions he faced. The two talked for about three minutes and then ended with the man in my presence praying for the one on the other end of the line. I noticed especially that the prayer did not in any way try to elicit a particular answer but merely asked that God would bring forth His own perfect will.

It was an interesting way to run an agency. The tone of Washington may be getting sweeter.

As I walked down the hallway, I wondered what the A.C.L.U. would do if it knew some of our government's most effective workers were praying about their decisions, just as the founding fathers of the nation had done.

★ ★ ★ ★ ★ ★ ★ ★ ★ ★ ★ ★ *10* ★ ★ ★ ★ ★ ★ ★ ★ ★ ★ ★ ★ ★

The White House

STRUGGLING WITH THE ISSUE of whether a man of Reagan's convictions can govern a nation of disparate people like the United States, we've touched on the atmosphere of the world, the country, and the national capital. But what about the residence of presidential power itself, the White House? What is the spiritual and political temper there?

The average person tends to think it's the same as that of the head man. After all, he's the boss. But is it?

Good books are not constructed of unattributed information. The same should hold true for newspaper, television, and magazine reports. But certainly writers of books, which are expected to be more permanent than the shorter vehicles that are constantly battling against time and space, should find ways to report their sources.

However, in cases like the one at hand, careful consideration convinces me that the following interview, with the White House party unidentified, provides understanding beyond that of a synopsis in which the author simply takes the credit for the information. The language of conversation can give added insight. Suffice it to say that the person, interviewed prior to changes in the White House staff in October, 1983, speaks from experience, authority, and dedication to the President of the United States.

Question: I need some insight as to the atmosphere around the White House.

Answer: Well, this White House, as any White House is, I'm sure—some more than others—is a very intense place in which to work. And it is fraught with all the problems that come with a vast collection of people who deal with all the strengths and weaknesses of human nature.

There are turf battles, there are ego trips, there are differences of philosophy, different priorities—just sometimes lack of understanding because of the complexity of a big operation that moves so fast that the right hand doesn't know what the left hand is doing or doesn't understand.

So you learn to work with your back to the wall and to cover yourself as best you can in case somewhere down the road you have to be sure that someone else understands that you didn't do something that you shouldn't have done, or that you did do something that you should have done, and so on.

And I think that's true of any White House.

I think in this day and age when we have such very intense struggles going on between two conflicting value systems—between secular humanism on one hand and the Judeo-Christian principles and faith on the other hand— you're going to have that struggle go on in all the fabric of our society, and the White House is not exempt from it. And so we do have some of that here.

There are occasions, because I have some very strong Christian views and—I can't speak for the president—but it appears to me that we share pretty much the same views, in that area. I have on occasion, in some meetings, felt like the skunk in the garden party. Sometimes, when people who think of things only in terms of political support, realize that your views are held by a number of key supporters in the country, sometimes you're the *honored* skunk, but you're very much aware of that.

Question: Why, when you have a president who feels as strongly as he does, not only about Christianity, but morality and ethics in general—why does this still go on just as in any other White House?

Answer: Because not everyone feels as he does and not everyone does put politics secondary to the principles.

Question: Why are they there?

Answer: I wish I knew the answer to that question.

It's very difficult to be in a position of leadership and have a large, large staff—and to become president of the country and have a staff as enormous as his really is and to deal with all the various national and international issues that come at him all the time. It would be difficult to be totally in touch with everything that goes on up and down his staff. He's a good administrator because he does assign responsibilities and then he lets go of them, and then he puts his trust in the judgment of those people that bring back to him for final decision many of the various items that they have been delegated the responsibility for. He also is a very trusting man, and he likes people. It's hard for this president to think ill of anyone else. Someone that he likes, and someone that he knows—he has a hard time really understanding that they don't always do things that he would like to have them do. And— he likes people so much.

Question: I've had lots of good conversation with people about the three or four that at least the world thinks of as the top people in the White House—Meese, Baker, Deaver, Clark—and they believe they would say those people believe in God. Now, at the same time, they acknowledge that there is a bit of the politicking going on—the turf situation and all of that—but they still believe the guys immediately around the president are at least nominally Christians.

Answer: I think that's right. I know that Judge Clark is—I know, I think that—I believe Jim [Baker] is a Christian—yes, I do, I know he is. Mike Deaver was in the seminary, I understand, at one point in time [He did not actually attend seminary, although he reportedly considered it]—that's all I know. Meese—you know about.

Question: I've asked numerous people why Mike Deaver appears to be one of the guys the president really likes to be around.

Answer: I don't know. I've thought about that, and there are a few other people—[Reagan's] personal friends—I've thought about. Then I think of some of the personal friends in my life, from long standing, that I really like a lot, but I don't agree with in most anything, and probably some of my Christian friends, were they to meet them, would wonder what I see in them.

There is something of value, of course, and something to really like in everybody. You just have to look further in some than others.

There's a difference in believing in God and in trusting Him—in believing in God's existence, and maybe even having made a personal commitment for salvation, and in believing in God's Word, in that it works today and that He moves among and through men today, in the affairs of nations. There's a big difference—that [latter] is a much deeper step of faith. Now I think the president has gone much further down that path than some of the people around him. But you hear all these voices in the world and all these voices have—the political world is saying, "Now you've got to do this." The world of politics is manipulative. You make things happen, and you shrewdly move things around—it's a head strategy game. That means you've got to be in control—and when you do things God's way, you have to let Him be in control. That's really hard to do, especially when you think, "Boy, I've got not only the fate of the country, but of the world in my hands," or "I'm advising the guy who does." And then you have all these worldly, practical worldly voices coming at you all the time, or ridiculing you, or looking down its nose—and you live within this, whatever they call it, sixty-eight square miles, bounded by reality, here in the Beltway—and people talk about—you know, their daily news is what happened in the White House and the Congress—is politics.

A great share of the people that do most of the talking and get most of the attention out here, or shape the news from within the media, don't believe the way this president believes, and that's all you hear. You've got to go out and find out where real America lives and how they think in order to get—to keep your head on straight. A lot of people here don't have enough time or the inclination to do that, or know the need to do it. Therefore, it creates a false climate, plus I think this spiritual dimension of—I think there's spiritual warfare going on in this country, and I think it's logically centered over this place.

Question: I know you can't judge—you can't tell people's hearts—you really don't know their faith except as you see it through the Spirit working in them, but at the risk of sounding judgmental, can you—how many believers are there around in key positions in the White House staff?

Answer: That's really hard. A minority . . . there is salt all around.

Discussions with knowledgeable people at several levels in the White House staff and with others in the administration supported the descriptions and tone of this interview.

There is extraordinary loyalty to the president at every turn, and support of most of his principles is widespread, although not always unanimous. A significant number also hold to his spiritual convictions, although not all are comfortable in talking about them.

And that takes us to one of the exceptional facts about this presidency and the way this White House works. Probably the most persuasive factor in Ronald Reagan's Christian life, at work and elsewhere, is its unpretentiousness. Everyone interviewed who has had contact with him speaks of it. He has a manner of raising spiritual points, perhaps interjecting a biblical idea, in such an offhand, unreligious way that it seems very natural. Few take offense. This occurs sometimes at Cabinet meetings, in sessions with senior advisers, over the dinner table, in speeches. It seems to roll out in a manly, sometimes rough, unpolished way, blending right into the context—artless and uncontrived.

That, most observers agree, is the most convincing evidence of his sincerity. Not even the most hardened seem tempted to say that he "doth protest too much."

Ed Meese, one of the president's closest advisers, made a subtle, but noticeable correction of one of my leading remarks during a quiet discussion one Saturday morning. I noted that Reagan seemed to be a sincere man, a Christian, and that he "wants that to underlie the things that he does in his life."

Meese interjected, "More than *wants* to; I think it *does.*"

He looked squarely into my face. "It's an interesting thing. The president is a very spiritually oriented person, but he has been scrupulously careful not to flaunt that or to use it in a way that would allow it to appear that he's using it for self-serving or political reasons."

He paused ever so slightly, leaning forward in his easy chair. "At the same time, I've been tremendously impressed that he can talk about his religious convictions without any feeling of embarrassment or even a reticence that the average person has. A lot of this is because of his sincerity—more than any other man I've ever met—he's the same person inside and out that he is with the public. I mean, he doesn't have two personalities—one in public and one in private."

A smile played on his lips and he looked at his fingers clasped in front of him for a second, then added, "Obviously you're able to be more candid and more frank in private than you could be in public, but there's no real change in approach or personality. And he will talk as spontaneously about religious matters as he will anything else in almost a matter-of-fact way, which is extremely refreshing."

Discussions with numerous others who have been in positions to observe the style of the president and those around him produced several anecdotes illustrating such spontaneous remarks.

"He's a very private person," one said, "and he doesn't talk a lot about his faith, at least in a religious way. But he says oblique things sometimes when faced with questions, things like 'I'll have to talk to the man upstairs,' and so on."

Another significant remark came in a session on the budget at Camp David. "During debate on a key point," one recalled, "the president said something like 'When I spoke to my "first counselor" about it, He told me not to do it.' "

Still others noted the ease and appropriateness with which Reagan quoted from Scripture when referring publicly to the heroism of people following a tragic airline accident along the Potomac in February of 1982. "We had this speech written for him when he went to New York," recalled Ben Elliott, chief presidential speechwriter, "and this thing happened after the speech was finished, late in the afternoon— everything had gone. And the next morning, we were wondering what he was going to say. And he, in his own words, wrote something going up on that plane, and it was, 'Greater love hath no man than this, that a man lay down his life for his friends.' That's right out of John [15:31]. And he didn't say, 'I want you to know that the Bible says.' He just *said* it."

It was natural, a part of the moment, a part of the man.

Elliot added this piece of insight: "He doesn't want to be preachy, because then he feels like he is setting up religion itself to be criticized, as opposed to taking the truth of the message and making that to be the criteria of what is judged."

My talks, long and short, with many people revealed that the matter-of-fact, natural way of voicing religious truth is not commonplace among the White House staff. And that should surprise no one. Americans have been drilled for years in the notion that the secular and spiritual are not to be mixed. We can go to church on the weekend if we want to, but we are to park all those Judeo-Christian ideas on the shelf as we go about our business during the rest of the week.

Nonetheless, the president's convictions appeared to be shared, if rather silently, by a number of his close advisers. The inner circle, called the Big Three or Big Four at various stages, seemed to be made up of men of some Christian conviction. In addition, a high percentage of the twenty or so making up the senior staff also professed at least *some* faith in God, ranging from nominal churchgoing to deep commitment. "I think every one of these guys would say he's a Christian," one high administration official reported, but he was equally certain that the majority would be speaking out of a cultural experience, not a spiritual one.

Conversations inside and outside the White House confirmed these views, although without question it is impossible for another human to determine such matters conclusively. The Scriptures say God looks upon the heart, and that's where these issues are decided. But the Scriptures also say faith should produce fruit and good works, and thus some external conclusions are possible.

For much of the time, especially in the administration's middle eighteen months of relative stability and confidence, the Big Four at the White House were, alphabetically, Baker, Clark, Deaver, and Meese. Power, at least as the popular press reported it, seemed to ebb and flow from office to office and from period to period. First Meese was the kingpin, as we read it, then Baker, then Clark. Then Clark was suddenly gone—to be Secretary of the Interior in place of the controversial James Watt, who resigned under fire over his blunt remarks. Deaver, meanwhile, remained consistently close to the president personally. In truth, the power among the Big Four probably remained at fairly consistent levels, at least as far as President Reagan was concerned, although Clark unquestionably rose to a level of extraordinary influence midway through the four-year term as mastery of his job grew.

During this important period, Clark, as National Security Adviser, concerned himself with foreign and defense affairs, which was a new area for the former judge. Meese dealt primarily in domestic policy. Baker was chief of the White House staff. And Deaver was Baker's deputy. But crossover in activities was frequent, especially among Meese, Baker, and Deaver—the original Big Three. Little occurred that they weren't in some way involved in. In the critical phase of the administration's stabilization and maturation—the third and fourth years—their power was great, as was Clark's during much of that time.

From all accounts, Clark and Meese reflected the thinking of Reagan—in almost every way—more closely than all others, with the exception of Mrs. Reagan. Years of togetherness in California and in Washington had caused them to see things the same way. All observers were agreed that Clark and Meese, above any of the senior staffers and often in conflict with a number of them, were committed to "letting Reagan be Reagan" instead of engaging in political gamesmanship.

And this similarity of thought included many spiritual as well as political, international, and social policy perspectives, not that this spiritual kinship had been planned at the start of their relationships. This simply was the way it was.

Clark—rancher, lawyer, gubernatorial chief of staff, state supreme court justice, deputy secretary of state, and then White House foreign affairs and national security specialist for a crucial period in the development of the Reagan White House—is a serious Roman Catholic. He hasn't been exposed in a major way to the evangelicalism of some of his colleagues, and he is not overly pious. But "the judge" has an unostentatious belief in the Lord that has been a part of his individualistic life for many years. He is not unfamiliar with the Bible. Prayer, usually private, is part of his existence. By his own admission, his Christian life has consisted primarily of a vertical relationship with God and very little horizontal relationship with other members of the body of Christ. In the words of a colleague, he tends to cloister himself, in his work, in his life. He works hard and keeps to himself. "You don't know where he's coming from," said a friend, "because he does it alone. He keeps things inside of him. He's not a joiner."

People who know and understand the Reagan White House emphasized that despite his voluntary shift to a Cabinet post, Clark would remain unusually influential in presidential matters beyond Interior business. He was one of those completely dedicated to serving Reagan in whatever specific job needed doing, but in the broad arena of general policy he still thought like the president and was a valued all-around adviser when the chips were down. As for his successor, Robert C. McFarlane, he was expected to continue the tone set by Clark. Perceptive White House advisers were confident that things "will continue pretty much as they have" since McFarlane, like Clark, is a tough conservative who keeps a low personal profile. Spiritually, he fits, too, acknowledged by the president himself to be "God-fearing," although maintaining a typical degree of privacy regarding his relationship with the Lord. All that he would say publicly was that he is a Protestant.

Meese—legal affairs specialist, policy thinker, cabinet member, counselor to the president—is an active Lutheran. More affable and outgoing than Clark, he is comfortable with evangelicals, in part because of his long-standing relationship with Herb Ellingwood, director of the Merit Systems Protection Board, an outspoken Christian leader in California, Washington, and around the country generally. Meese—who is joined in his Christian commitment by his wife, Ursula—participates in at least one weekly Bible study group and is quite familiar with the Scriptures. A few close friends feel that his dependence upon Christ, and his openness regarding it, has deepened during his White House years, possibly because of the accidental death of a son. Meese himself does not acknowledge a great deal of change in his ongoing Christian life other than that he has become more visible to the public and "they may recognize it more."

Baker—chief of staff, political strategist—is a newcomer to the California group, having managed George Bush's bid for the Republican presidential nomination in 1980 before joining up with the Reagan forces. He is politically astute in the conventional sense, and the so-called "pragmatism" resulting from that has cost him popularity with many of the president's religious and politically conservative supporters. This has tended to diminish recognition of both his Christian commitment and his conservative politics. But the lanky Texas lawyer, an Episcopalian, married to an openly committed Christian, is known to be a man of occasional prayer and Bible reading, sharp political motivations notwithstanding. And on matters of principle he is not far from the president, despite a reputation for willingness to bend principle in a rush of expediency.

Deaver—technically Baker's deputy but in practice more than that—is perhaps the most intriguing of the four. He, too, is a man with an underlying belief in the Lord. He is an Episcopalian who prays and knows something of the Bible. Yet he bears the reputation of one with a sort of quick-witted irreverence and worldliness that stand out among his rather staid peers. It may be this, it may be his loyalty and willingness to serve, it may be his anticipation of the needs of the Reagans—but something quite intangible elevates him to the position of one whom President and Mrs. Reagan enjoy being around. He, unlike most others, is sometimes invited to the president's residential quarters. He has influence.

A number of people in the administration voice bafflement over the origin of Deaver's power. But those who have known him and the Reagans for many years say the relationship is a simple, logical one. Years ago, he was assigned as sort of "keeper of the body" for the president. If Reagan wanted something, it was Deaver's responsibility. If Mrs. Reagan wanted something, it was also his responsibility. This could include travel needs, a party, security concerns, even "homework for the kids," one friend said. Deaver was a good servant, all concluded.

Some said he had no axes to grind; he was thoroughly committed to the president. Others felt that eventually, in the White House years, a concern for personal power evolved. "He would like to see himself as much more sophisticated than circumstances call for," one official said. Spiritually, that person added, he may not be on the same wavelength as the president, but he's not moving contrary to it.

An examination of the way the White House works showed this:

Early in the administration, Meese, Baker, and Deaver met every morning over breakfast. As they and their staff matured in their jobs, they changed that meeting to once a week, at 7:30 A.M., to compare schedules, brief one another, and attempt to anticipate problems.

At 8 o'clock every morning, they met with the senior staff—the assistants to the president and a few others who make up that group of about twenty. At 8:30, the three met separately with their top four or five people, primarily to run over the things on the agenda for that day.

Then at 9 A.M., Baker, Meese, and Deaver met with the president, briefing him on the day's schedule, reviewing overnight developments, in general keeping him fully informed on events and, in turn, hearing the matters foremost on his mind. At 9:30, Clark (now McFarlane) and Vice President George Bush joined the group for a national security briefing. This was led by Clark or a member of his staff, or perhaps by the Secretary of State, George Shultz, an ambassador or a State Department specialist. Those attending and the agenda were determined for the most part by events.

At 9:45, Baker, Meese, and Deaver were free to bring in any of their senior aides to brief the president and the others on important matters.

By 10 o'clock each day, the president and the key White House aides, with that series of meetings, had at least a working knowledge of national and international matters facing the country. Although there was continual give-and-take throughout the day, they for the most part went their own ways after that to follow through on action items that might have come from the sessions and to proceed with their staffs and ongoing activities.

Important in White House operations, obviously, were Cabinet functions, with two formats. There was the full group of department secretaries plus the handful of Cabinet-level aides, who met weekly, if not more often. Then there were the seven Cabinet Councils that group the Cabinet officers according to subject matter—human resources, natural resources, economic affairs, and the like. An eighth grouping was the National Security Council.

The president did not formally attend the Cabinet Council meetings that were purely planning or study sessions in which options and ideas were explored. But he attended those, averaging about one a month, where decisions were made or final options presented. Those usually dealt with major policy questions that ultimately incorporated expertise right across the government and outside where necessary.

At the White House, questions and issues originated in various ways, as with any organization facing day-to-day, as well as long-range, operations. Daily events in the nation and the world were responsible for many of these. The president originated some, as did various governmental departments and agencies and White House policy planners.

For example, all White House people overseeing any part of policy— the chairman of the Council of Economic Advisers, the director of Science and Technology, the head of the Office of Policy Development, the head of the Office of Cabinet Affairs, and the like—met weekly. At that time came early warnings of things on the horizon or perhaps just beyond the horizon. Appropriate people were assigned to inject advance planning into the system, which would in important cases reach the Cabinet level and the president's attention ultimately.

Through all of this, Meese and Clark (now McFarlane), along with Baker and Deaver at certain points, served essentially as coordinators, striving to see that all avenues were covered. They did not themselves originate all matters that flowed to the Cabinet and the president. But they were gatekeepers and shepherds, and thus exercised massive responsibility.

Lesser categories of decision-making followed various courses, although the similarity of, one, a brief meeting with the president, and, two, delegation to the appropriate people was found in most White House activities.

Personnel decisions were made for the most part in the following manner: Meese, Baker, and Deaver met once a week for an hour, usually on Wednesday afternoons, with the Office of Presidential Personnel. Recommendations for personnel decisions were laid out for review. If the three had questions they could not resolve, these were taken to the president, usually at a half-hour meeting the following day, and he made or approved the decisions. One or more of the threesome usually sat in on this meeting, which also considered certain high-level ambassadorial decisions that went through not only Presidential Personnel but also the State Department.

Scheduling decisions—where the president went, what he did—while basically handled by Deaver, nonetheless received input from Meese and Baker, quite often in the early morning meetings. This area of activity was the primary source of Deaver's power at the White House, of course. The president's day-to-day activities, including social activities and events at the White House residence, were important not only to the Reagans but also to the nation. The matter of whom the president saw, for example, could deeply influence his thinking, which in turn could affect the course of a significant event or policy. The impact of this was further extended by Deaver's responsibility for the First Lady's activities and requirements.

As we've seen, Meese's unique impact, while broad and far-ranging, was most heavily felt in areas of policy and future courses for the administration. His responsibilities and interests touched many departments and agencies across the land, which gave him extraordinary influence, particularly in the long term. Reagan respected Meese's ability to pull together many diverse channels in arriving at policy recommendations. He also respected his long-proven integrity in presenting the full spectrum of options, even those that Meese himself disagreed with. This capacity for even-handedness, plus the natural inclination to think like Reagan, created vast power.

Baker's power, on the other hand, flowed in three veins essentially. First, he was responsible for the administrative machinery of the White House. This put him in touch with everything. Second, he was directly responsible for every area in the White House with a communications function, whether with outside groups, the political community, or the media. Third, he had charge of the legislative activities of the White House. His people continually dealt with Capitol Hill, although Meese and Deaver—and others, including the president—functioned in this realm only from time to time. Any one of those activities carried power; put together they generated enormous clout.

As for Clark's power, he operated much like Meese, as we've seen, although his field—national security—was more concentrated, despite the fact that it can involve the entire world. Defense, foreign affairs, intelligence policy, relations with Moscow—all were overwhelming. They could touch the very fabric of the United States and thus called for awesome power. Clark had it. McFarlane was in the process of earning it.

While all of the president's senior advisers were in many ways like-minded, some were more so than others. Among the top four, during the crucial middle years, this seemed to produce two groups, although they did not overtly break into such pairings. Meese and Clark seemed to fit together, as did Baker and Deaver, who were joined quite naturally in their affinity of goals and tactics by powerful members of their staffs. David Gergen, director of communications, slipped quite comfortably into the Baker-Deaver style. So did Richard Darman, another Baker assistant, who dealt in administration.

Given the obvious similarities of the Meese-Clark and Baker-Deaver attitudes—loyalty to Reagan; commitment to turning the country around, at least to some degree; belief for the most part in basically traditional, sometimes Judeo-Christian values—what were the differences? And did they matter?

The most obvious had to do with tactics. Clark and Meese were policy people. Baker and Deaver were politicians. This caused the first two and their coterie to want Reagan to be Reagan—firm, principled and even idealistic, aggressive in what he believed to be right, true to his campaign commitments. Baker and Deaver, plus their followers, tended toward conventional political wisdom and thus stood somewhat in awe of the political establishment. Like their boss, they're Westerners, but they were tempted by Eastern power games. Responsible for dealing with Congress and the press, they were willing to be more accommodating with the political nation, the system, than a number of their critics believed was good for the president or the country. Their strongest detractors feared they were willing to sacrifice principle. Their admirers said no, they merely knew how to get things done.

A number of informed people drew a parallel between the philosophy and methods of this "political" portion of the White House senior staff and those of John Sears, who ran Reagan's campaigns in 1976 and part of 1980. They were quick to point out, however, that Sears, who had worked for Richard Nixon, was not really a conservative. Baker and Deaver are.

But Sears was noted for his "pragmatism," his concern with the Eastern liberal establishment within the GOP, his lack of deep conviction that a conservative could be elected and could govern. He would not let Reagan be Reagan. He was overly concerned with the press. It was in these areas that Baker-Deaver detractors drew parallels. The detractors especially pointed to a number of people who worked for Baker and Deaver.

These differences in the senior staff produced sporadic press reports of serious clashes within the White House operation. Because of the spiritual and ethical emphasis of the Reagan administration, it was important to track down the reports. Persistent discussions produced the following synopsis of opinion:

The clash was not as intense and pervasive as published reports contended. There were difficulties from time to time. Mostly they derived from those accustomed to "the Washington power game," which included use of the media "to enhance one person and cut up another." Some staffers, even those loyal to Reagan, were willing to play that game, but a significant number were not. Occasionally two "games" were actually underway. Players in one game were bent on putting every piece of the Reagan program into place, foreign and domestic, and players in the other game were overcome by long-term political and personal ambition, which necessitated a deep concern with the Eastern establishment. One group of players had its eyes upon eventually returning home and resuming previous occupations. The other group had its eyes upon Washington and New York and the avenues they provided; thus reputation was important.

Not often, but occasionally, when mistakes were made or things went badly for the administration, there was scurrying to exonerate oneself and subtly direct the blame elsewhere. This created moments of divisiveness and tension. It hurt the president. Some observers said it might have contributed to Clark's readiness to go to Interior.

Frequently, the ones at the center of the aggravation were not the principals themselves, but subordinates who saw profit for themselves in trying to make their bosses look good.

A surprisingly significant factor in the operation of the White House, often unnoticed by those of us accustomed to traditional political practices, has been the role of Vice President Bush.

Perhaps even more important to the atmosphere than his actual functions, which have been substantial, has been the concord between Bush and Reagan. This caught a number of the forecasters off guard, for in 1980 these two onetime competitors seemed poles apart. But observation and reflection show this speculation to have been superficial. It was based far too much on their rhetoric rather than intimate knowledge of the beliefs of the two men.

In fact, Reagan and Bush themselves did not know immediately that they would develop the kind of respect for one another that has evolved. They, too, had listened to the rhetoric.

An examination of day-to-day operations shows that Bush, in addition to presiding over the Senate, attends every major White House meeting, particularly those of the Cabinet, the National Security Council, and the Cabinet Councils. He participates actively, although virtually never putting himself in the limelight, according to others attending the same sessions.

In addition, he meets a minimum of once a week with the president privately over lunch, and they are thrown together in small and large groups throughout the week. Bush has been particularly useful to the administration in intelligence and foreign affairs because of his background as head of the Central Intelligence Agency, ambassador to the United Nations, and ambassador to China. But his additional service as a congressman from Texas and as chairman of the Republican National Committee have provided expertise in numerous domestic matters also.

Among the special assignments he has undertaken for the president are:

—Representing Reagan in Atlanta during the crisis over the murder of black children.

—Heading the South Florida task force on narcotics control, a top priority item in the president's war on organized crime.

—Overseeing the national narcotics border interdiction system.

—Heading the deregulation task force.

—Heading the special situation corps, known as the Crisis Management Control Group.

—Representing the President in Lebanon after the terrorist bombing that killed 239 Marines and other servicemen.

Each of these activities represents an important component in the Reagan administration's efforts to deal with problems that had approached crisis levels in its long-range planning. According to one strategically placed observer, Bush undertook each of the tasks with zeal and with intelligence.

That observer, questioned about the personal closeness of Reagan and Bush, in the execution of their jobs, in light of their seemingly different backgrounds, said the following: "If you in all honesty look at Bush's positions in Congress, they were not consistently those of the liberal Republican mainstream, but tended toward the conservative. In foreign affairs, intelligence, and security matters, his positions were usually close to those taken by the president. The differences—perhaps in domestic issues—were not big; many of the things the president has moved forward on, George had not taken positions on before."

This source reiterated the well-reported fact that when Bush accepted the vice-presidential nomination in 1980, he committed himself to following and working for Reagan's programs. "He obviously meant it," the observer said.

As we've noted, unity is important to Reagan as a man. The California governorship and the campaign proved this. He cannot stand acrimony and dissension, although he allows and welcomes differences of opinion on his staff and in the Cabinet. He and a number of his close aides believe staff disagreement and conflict of the kind discussed earlier is good, but they expect expression of those differences to remain within the group, not to find its way into newspapers and television reports, nor to be spread around the Washington cocktail circuit.

But the president, who is neither a grudge carrier nor vindictive, has trouble correcting or disciplining those who let him down. Like many secular and religious leaders, personal confrontation is not his favorite tactic. He much prefers to have people like him.

Therefore, he has been slow in his first presidential years to acknowledge division when it has appeared and slower still to cut it off. A number of his close friends addressed this when they noted that kindness may be his biggest problem. He was forced, however, on one or two occasions to gather his top aides in a room and order them to settle their differences and to stop leaking their feelings to the press. Their obedience was mixed.

As Governor of California, primarily because of inexperience and in some cases ignorance, Reagan grew overly dependent upon his staff in the early years. He delegated a lot, which is still his favorite style, and he appeared to carry it a bit far, again showing a reluctance to confront subordinates. In the second term, he grew stronger and was much more in control.

As president, he showed similar tendencies of overdelegation in the foreign policy area in the first twelve months. His delegation and

The President enjoys a light moment in the Oval Office. (Michael
Evans—The White House)

President and Mrs. Reagan gaze across the White House lawns.
(Bill Fitz-Patrick—The White House)

Reagan embraces Nhanny Heil, the Vietnamese girl found in a box. Mrs. Reagan reaches toward Nhanny's adoptive mother as the father looks on. (Pete Souza—The White House)

Mrs. Reagan chats with Mother Teresa in President's residence. (Michael Evans—The White House)

Defense Secretary Caspar Weinberger (left) and National Security Advisor William P. Clark (now Secretary of the Interior) brief the President at the Oval Office desk. (Mary Anne Fackelman— The White House)

Reagan interrupts Oval Office lunch with Vice President Bush to answer a call. (Mary Anne Fackelman—The White House)

A moment of banter precedes opening of meeting of school prayer leaders. From left to right are the Reverend Jerry Falwell, the President, Bishop Thomas Welsh, and Connaught Marshner. Among the observers are Dee Jepsen (second from left), former Special Assistant to the President for Public Liaison. (Jack Kightlinger—The White House)

Shortly after the attempt on his life in 1981, Ronald Reagan chats with Terence Cardinal Cooke of New York, an important figure in the President's life. Cardinal Cooke succumbed to cancer in the fall of 1983. (Michael Evans—The White House)

Billy Graham accepts the Medal of Freedom from the President.
(Mary Anne Fackelman—The White House)

Prime Minister Thatcher listens intently in a serious moment
at the White House. (Michael Evans—The White House)

Former Prime Minister Menachem Begin of Israel and President Reagan stand at attention during ceremony on White House lawn. (Michael Evans—The White House)

Five powerful men confer in the Oval Office, left to right: Edwin Meese III, James A. Baker III, William P. Clark, Michael K. Deaver, and President Reagan. (Michael Evans—The White House)

Reagan rides with friends at his California ranch. (Mary Anne
Fackelman—The White House)

detachment became unwieldy, and wobbly moments resulted. The unity of the Big Three of Meese, Baker, and Deaver faltered, Richard V. Allen found himself in trouble as national security adviser and departed, Bill Clark came in, and Secretary of State Alexander Haig was soon gone.

The lesson for Reagan was that he must intervene with his staff more than he had, that he must be involved more directly in the execution of policy, that he must continue to learn on the job. A figurehead role would not suffice—nor was it what he truly wanted.

Still, despite improvement in his performance, unity remained an elusive link in what he wanted to accomplish. To succeed with his long-range goals, he must have it. It's a spiritual principle, and it's a secular principle: The world and its components respond favorably to unity; they crumble under disunity.

Given the Christian beliefs of a number of Reagan's top aides, one wonders why the senior White House people, when their infrequent clashes break into the open, do not resort to the time-tested practice of prayer to overcome differences. I asked one of them, "Do you guys ever do anything as far out as pray together?"

"No, we haven't," he replied. "That has never come up. . . . We have prayed together on occasion, such as when we were in the chapel after the president was shot, and when we went to church service with him prior to inauguration. I mean, we happened to be in a prayerful situation at the same time—but as far as having prayer together, we do not."

I asked another administration official whether it would be possible for key people around the president to pray together about issues and conflicts. He responded quickly: "You'd have to have people around who respected that," implying his opinion that such was not the case at the moment. "They would have to understand what the world would think—the criticism, the mockery."

Without hesitating, he added his own attitude toward praying by national leaders: "It's the only way. There are no solutions—environmental controls, world diplomacy, whatever. We're going to have to come to that."

A key contributor to the atmosphere at the White House is Nancy Reagan. She creates atmosphere. And, for the president, she calms it.

Few people in the political world seem to know Mrs. Reagan the way they feel they do the president. Yet all are agreed that her influence, while exercised far differently from that of past president's wives, is widespread.

To begin with, she is shy. And that contributes in natural ways to her preference for privacy and general disdain for public forums. She also prefers the company of personal friends, many of whom are wealthy, to the political circles she has often been thrust into over the last twenty years. But because "Ronnie" likes politics, she likes politics, or at least she supports him in his likes.

One who knows and likes both the president and Nancy provided this observation of their relationship:

"He is her leader and she looks up to him, and she not only is his support system, but he'd have a hard time without Nancy. She's a tremendously important person to him, but she depends on him—like leaning two things together and holding them both up."

As for the sharing of their Christian faith, the friend said:

"I don't know that there was any religious training in the home—at least that I'm aware of. I don't know that she has any [close] friends who are committed Christians. I think he is the spiritual leader in that marriage, and she's leaning on that. And I know there are a lot of people who are praying for her.

"I know that her father's death was very upsetting to her. She loved him dearly and, really, it was very hard, because I know she is very sensitive, and I know there were some people who tried to give her spiritual support and a spiritual message at that time. (Shortly before the death of her father, actually her stepfather, Loyal Davis, Reagan wrote to him about eternal life through faith in Jesus Christ, obviously with the acquiescence of Nancy.)

"I know that [the president] has, in the presence of another prominent Christian leader, talked very extensively about a commitment to Christ and what it means to be born again—in her presence—and I'm sure that he hopes that's where she is."

As for the public Mrs. Reagan:

"She's a very shy lady, and so therefore they [White House aides] protect her, as well they should, and it's hard for people to know how to make initiatives to her."

Another friendly White House staffer, asked for insight into Nancy's Christian life in relation to the president's, said this immediately: "She certainly doesn't stand in the way, that's for sure!"

Then reflecting a bit more, the person added: "She finds it personally difficult to express things in a personal way the way he does. That's not her forte. But that, I don't think, is an indication that she doesn't feel in her heart that what he says is right and she agrees with him. I know she told the story when he was shot about how her daughter, Patti, was very angry, when he came home, about this guy Hinckley and how—I don't know what the word was, whether she wanted him shot or put away or what—and the president turned around and said, 'God loves him as much as He does us.' And Nancy just kind of threw it away, but she told that story as an example of the great guy she's married to, and indicated in the telling that she agreed."

Many Washington observers of the Reagans are not convinced, however, that Nancy's commitment to Christ is as encompassing as the president's. They describe her as "an awfully nice, good, and compassionate woman," but from moderately close observation, some of them question whether her faith goes beyond a cultural, social Christianity.

To understand Nancy Reagan, her private manner, and her public manner, it helps to remember that this attractive, poised, wealthy woman comes from an early childhood of great insecurity and unhappiness. She suffered deeply as the offspring of a short-lived marriage of a stage actress and a car salesman. She was forced at the age of two to live with an aunt and uncle in Bethesda, Maryland.

From a life of some deprivation, she was thrust into a life of luxury and privilege when her mother, Edith Luckett, married a prominent and successful Chicago neurosurgeon, Loyal Davis. The unhappy days vanished immediately, but not the memories. So she clutched the life of fashionable surroundings, good schools, and debutante parties to her relentlessly. She needed security.

To her, Loyal Davis was father, and her name was legally changed from Anne Frances Robbins to Nancy Davis. She acknowledged no other father, and she cherished the life he prepared her to lead. Only Ronald Reagan has been able to compete, apparently, and the life he has provided has not necessitated deviation from her desired standard.

An admittedly biased observer and friend, Shirley Boone, reflected on Mrs. Reagan, her faith, and her ways. "You know, the thing I love most about Nancy as a woman—" a smile broke across her face "—I mean, I'm looking at her now in this position and not as a friend or as a school board member, and all the things that you did at school when you're running the hotdog stands and you're in your blue jeans, running all over making paper flowers to cover the cyclone fence, and all those normal things. The thing I love is she's silent in her dignity of being a wife. She speaks very loudly, with no words, of her being a helpmeet, of her really being an undergirding power behind President Reagan. But I don't think she has to say it with words. This woman speaks with unspoken words—things that women need to see and hear in today's hour because the support that she gives him is maybe more important than all the supposed ideas that president's wives have on whether they decorate the White House properly or whether their charities have the approval of all the different people. But if she does nothing else in that office, she's brought a great dignity to the position, just being totally a wife."

Mrs. Boone said that in the late sixties "the Lord impressed" her to pray regularly for Nancy Reagan. This even preceded that Sunday afternoon in 1970 when the group prayed for the Reagans in Sacramento, sensing that they would one day be going to the White House.

"Now it's curious," she said, "that some women, the militant ones, say she's, well, a doormat, a Milquetoast or whatever. I've never found her to be that way—and she and I were on the school board together, and I watched her function as a board member and as a caring person. In fact, in a curious way, it's braver of her these days to do what she does and to take the supportive, undergirding, almost silent-partner role, than to go the other way. I really feel Nancy's ability in leadership is to be her own woman and to bring a dignity to the relationship of being a wife."

Knowledgeable people at the White House and elsewhere in the administration concurred to a large extent with Shirley Boone's assessment of Mrs. Reagan. Furthermore, although none was found who could speak with first-hand conviction, most agreed with the statement that "Mrs. Reagan probably feels somewhat, in terms of spiritual things and values, the way the president does." The Lord may or may not be the first one to come to mind when she awakens in the morning, but she does profess to believe in Him and holds a generally conservative, although not extremely well informed, view of the Bible.

As to influence in the workings of the White House, a well-placed aide said, "I think her influence is that of a good wife, because I think the president values her counsel, as many husbands do. But she does not interfere in the operations of the White House or try to exert influence on things nearly to the extent that the papers would like to portray. I think her influence is that she and her husband discuss things."

In the early days of the administration, Mrs. Reagan was the target of considerable press scorn. She was criticized as cold, aloof, concerned only for her wealthy friends. Reporters particularly could not tolerate what they described as "the gaze"—the frankly adoring way in which she stared at her husband no matter what he was doing.

Her standing with the media seemed to improve, however, in the administration's third year. For one thing, she was more relaxed. She adjusted to the political-governmental role. Official Washington became less intimidating. The papers picked up on that. But perhaps the most important development was her sincerity in the anti-drug campaign she espoused. She obviously cared and worked hard. Reporters became convinced.

One high-level administration official in a position to watch Mrs. Reagan's work to relieve national drug problems and to encourage adults in the difficulties of being parents in the late twentieth century said: "She has very strong feelings about kids staying away from the drug culture, and I think as her confidence has grown, based upon her knowledge that she's helping, this has made a difference. I've heard her speak—she doesn't speak long, but it's very moving, and it's heartfelt, and it's clear to me and the audience that this lady believes very strongly in it."

"I think what has happened," said a top White House person, "is that as the press has gotten to know her better and to know her as an individual, which they didn't at first, they have stopped prolonging the stereotype that they themselves created."

As becomes clear, the setting for the country's fortieth president in his determination to function as a conservative and a Christian has a multicolored backdrop. The outer tone is pretty much the same as his. But the texture of life as it is played out varies. And this influences his own performance.

His record shows a need for unity and harmony. Scripture says they're needed for meaningful success. This demands strong, like-minded staff people.

Many thoughtful observers believe that Jimmy Carter, operating from the other side of the political fence but nonetheless something of a populist at first and certainly an avowed Christian, began his slide to weakness as a president by surrounding himself with mediocre, uncommitted aides.

Unquestionably, atmosphere and ability at the White House are important. And there are other factors, as we will see.

★ ★ ★ ★ ★ ★ ★ ★ ★ ★ ★ ★ *11* ★ ★ ★ ★ ★ ★ ★ ★ ★ ★ ★ ★

The Visitors

RONALD REAGAN EXPERIENCES influence in still another fashion. The pressures from the world, the nation, the capital, and those people working in close proximity are evident, as we've seen— some good, some not so good, some merely confusing. As several White House Christians noted, "There are many voices." But an additional influence, it appears, fulfills an admonition from another man who underwent severe pressure from time to time—Paul, who flew in the face of the world and helped change it.

In what was probably the earliest-written of the books of the New Testament, Paul taught the Christians at Thessalonica how to view the death of loved ones prior to the return of Jesus, which the early believers thought was imminent. In doing so, he logically moved into some general instruction about the Second Coming, reminding them that "the day of the Lord will come like a thief in the night."[1] After encouraging them to alertness and to faith, hope and love, he set down a truth that followers of Jesus everywhere need to hear, especially today: "For God has not destined us for wrath, but to obtain salvation through our Lord Jesus Christ, who died for us so that whether we wake or sleep we might live with him."[2]

His point was that, yes, there would be severe pressure—tribulation—which should be recognized in its primary form as pressure on the spirit designed to drive us away from God. But that pressure, he implied, is not to cause us fear, since we will escape the wrath, the judgment, that will fall upon those rejecting the Lord Jesus.

And then came his insistence that Christians stand with one another, especially during the hard times ahead: "Therefore, encourage one another and build one another up, just as you are doing."[3]

134

And that, it seems, is a result, no matter how conscious the intent, of this additional influence that President Reagan is experiencing as he strives to govern the United States. He is receiving significant encouragement from Christians everywhere and especially from a number of highly respected individuals who have developed friendships with the Reagans over the years. I mentioned some of them in passing in chapter 4—Billy Graham, Donn Moomaw, Mother Teresa. They are "the visitors," the ones who through tested friendship have in fact been thrust into roles of building up and strengthening Ron and Nancy Reagan.

Ronald Reagan and Billy Graham met in the fifties. The movie actor's mother-in-law, Mrs. Loyal Davis, introduced them after encountering the fast-rising young evangelist at a golf course. Noting their mutual interests—presumably referring to their moral values and biblical, evangelical beliefs—she invited Graham in to meet Reagan. From that encounter blossomed a lasting friendship, proving once again that God can use anything—even an evangelist's passion for golf—to accomplish His purpose.

The friendship progressed a few months later when the two were co-speakers at an event scheduled to raise funds for a retirement home for actors. That led naturally to dinner together several times at the Reagans' home, producing an unusual but not unique affinity between two couples from quite different spheres of American society—the motion picture world and a crusade for men's souls. Conversation frequently centered on biblical subjects and their application to current life. Reagan and Graham each pressed the other on many points and it was sometimes difficult to distinguish which was the expert.

In the mid-sixties, the tie was modified. The actor became a politician and soon governor of the largest state in the Union. Their friendship continued and quite expectedly the evangelist was asked to speak to the state legislators on two occasions. At one time, he was invited to talk informally at a gathering of Cabinet members and a few other executives. The governor, betraying the keen interest in Bible prophecy that we saw in chapter 1, asked Graham to tell about Christ's second coming.

By this time Graham was one of the country's most popular personalities, with Gallup surveys showing that 72 to 88 percent of all Americans have held favorable opinions of him for the last twenty years. So it was not out of the ordinary for him to have numerous friends at the top levels of American politics, including several presidents, who seldom matched his high popularity ratings. Neither was it out of the ordinary for him and his wife, Ruth, to continue their relationship with Ron and Nancy when the latter's political horizons expanded from the state to the nation.

A person acquainted with the thinking of both Graham and Reagan related one anecdote describing this friendship at work at the national level. At the 1980 national convention, surrounded with controversy and a bit of bumbling over the selection of a running mate after he himself had secured the Republican nomination, Reagan ultimately chose George Bush. The next day, aware that the evangelist knew Bush, Reagan spoke by phone with Graham and told how he had been seeking guidance from the Lord when a forgotten incident involving Bush was brought to his mind.

"He knew Bush was the right man," this knowledgeable source said. He added, significantly, his certainty that this episode bore out the reports that Reagan prays, knows the Bible, and is guided by the Lord.

In the first two and a half years of the Reagan administration, Billy and Ruth Graham spent two nights at the White House. Again, the conversation, over dinner and into the evening, dealt frequently with spiritual, eternal matters.

On one of those occasions, Graham received the Medal of Freedom, the highest award that the country can bestow upon a civilian. It was a remarkable honor for a minister of the gospel.

As was noted in chapter 7, Graham was one of the religious leaders summoned immediately after the assassination attempt on the president. The Reagans' family pastor, Moomaw, as we saw, was vacationing outside the country and was delayed in reaching the president's bedside. Graham was called within two hours of the shooting.

Still another significant occasion that brought the Reagans and the Grahams together was the state dinner given for Britain's Queen Elizabeth in California during her visit to this country—again an extraordinary honor for an evangelist, even the world's foremost.

These times served to strengthen Reagan's already established biblical value system—Judeo-Christian in character—and to rekindle his personal commitment to base decisions on those values while remaining "progressive" and sensitive to the needs and aspirations of all people. Those in a position to observe this friendship and its results were convinced that Reagan had matured in his relationship with God to the point where he could maintain his ideology perhaps more than any predecessor and still function in a political world of pragmatism and compromise. They believed he had been reinforced in taking charge, remaining visibly and unequivocally so, refusing to compromise principle, yet responding to reason and logic posed by those differing with him. They did not use the terms, but they described a leader who possessed both "legal" and "spiritual" authority.

Mother Teresa of Calcutta, world renowned for her work among the poor and suffering, contributed a dimension to the shaping of the man in the White House, too. One visit made a strong, lasting impact upon both President and Mrs. Reagan. During a closed session with her, attended by only one or two others, both Reagans wept openly as they listened to the diminutive, strong-hearted woman in the nun's habit. Those who saw them emerge from the meeting said they had obviously been moved deeply.

In the discussions, the president, hearing the heart-rending stories of suffering among the poor, reportedly asked, in effect, "Mother Teresa, what can we do?"

The quiet little woman, whose soft words and persevering actions seem to speak so loudly, was said to have replied, "You could make some of the surplus food available to the poor."

After that dialogue, the president talked with the Secretary of Agriculture, John Block, to take steps among private groups to move toward that end.

Again, flesh-and-blood action flowed from faith.

We saw earlier how another Roman Catholic, the late Cardinal Cooke, touched Reagan at a critical time in his life. That relationship continued with other visits and took on even deeper overtones after the discovery of the archbishop's terminal illness. When the president went to New York in September, 1983, to address the United Nations, he and Mrs. Reagan visited the Cardinal and together prayed with him. The question of life or death in all its stark reality was an issue that bonded them together. They understood.

An even higher official within the Roman church, the pope himself, spent some time with the president and the effect on each was significant, according to White House observers.

Other well-known leaders who have touched the spiritual life at the White House at least to some degree are Jerry Falwell, founder of the Moral Majority; Bill and Vonette Bright of Campus Crusade; Louis Evans, Jr., pastor of the National Presbyterian Church; Richard

Halverson, chaplain of the Senate and pastor of the Fourth Presbyterian Church; and Pat Robertson, president of the Christian Broadcasting Network. The list goes on, but many tread so lightly as to leave few certain traces. Yet they number among those who provide encouragement in the manner urged by Scripture.

Another relationship between a pivotal White House figure and a Christian leader has flourished with little public awareness. Its importance to the United States is substantial.

Vice President George Bush and Billy Graham have been close friends for a long time, having first met more than thirty years ago. According to those acquainted with the affairs of both men, their relationship today is as strong, if not stronger, than any the evangelist has had with political figures throughout his ministry.

Graham was first a friend of George's father, Prescott, the senator. That developed into friendship between George and Billy and between their wives, Barbara and Ruth. Their families have also become quite close.

A person in a position to know rather intimate events within the families said that two or three of the Bush children have experienced life-changing commitments to Christ. It was not clear whether the experiences were a direct outgrowth of the relationship with the Grahams or had merely been enhanced by it.

The same informed source reported that the Vice President "very definitely" had made a personal commitment to the Lord and that his wife's "great interest" suggested the same experience.

Winter vacations with the Grahams in Mexico, summer weekends in Maine, visits in the Bushes' adopted home state of Texas, as well as in Washington, have at the very least served to nourish this embrace of God and His purpose for their lives. The Bushes, plus their children, have heard the plan of salvation, the possibilities of spiritual rebirth, and the realities of life "in Christ" from one of the world's leading authorities, a man and his wife whom they have grown to trust.

It became clear to all who knew them well that, without design, the Bushes' relationship with the Grahams was one of several influences drawing the president and the vice president closer together than any of the experts expected when they were elected in 1980. According to one senior White House figure, Reagan and Bush may have the closest presidential vice-presidential relationship in the history of the country.

Another source with even more intimate knowledge of the vice president's opinions declared, "Bush has tremendous appreciation for the president. He and his wife both speak of the Reagans in the highest terms." A person acquainted with both men reported that on more than one occasion Bush had said that "Ronald Reagan has had more influence on my life than any other man has."

The White House aide said the respect and high regard were reciprocated by the Reagans. "It's an amazingly warm relationship," he said—another of the several mysteries surrounding Ronald Reagan. It was especially baffling to the segment of society that we must now examine, the political nation.

★ ★ ★ ★ ★ ★ ★ ★ ★ ★ ★ ★ *12* ★ ★ ★ ★ ★ ★ ★ ★ ★ ★ ★ ★ ★

The Elite Minority

IN AMERICA, AS IN BRITAIN, stands an unusual impediment to the execution of the popular will. A number of thoughtful people have identified it and are writing and speaking about it with several variations. Yet the public has not caught on in any specific way, being only generally aware that matters have in some fashion been taken out of its hands.

Quite simply, there is the nation, which is the people, and there is the "political" nation, which runs things. Put another way, there is a common majority and an elite minority. Strangely, in this marvelous, democratic republic, the majority has not prevailed, at least for many years, certainly in the last twenty years.

It is thus possible for the nation to express its will, as it did, say, in the general election of 1980, and then to watch helplessly as that expression is opposed, pounded, and hammered almost to a standstill by this shadowy minority.

A professor at the London School of Economics, P. T. Bauer, wrote about this phenomenon with considerable restraint and clarity in *The Wall Street Journal* early in 1983:

> Mr. Heath (1970) and Mrs. Thatcher (1979) and Presidents Nixon (1972) and Reagan (1980) were elected by substantial majorities of the popular vote. However, they were elected without the support—indeed, with the opposition—of influential and articulate groups in the civil service, the academies and the media; and also against the wishes of "progressive" businessmen, politicized writers, critics, trade union leaders, clergymen, entertainers and professional humanitarians. Taken together, these categories largely make up the contemporary Western "political nation," that is the people who dominate discussion of public affairs, influence the course of events and circum-

scribe the freedom of the political leadership. What suits the interest of politicians is much influenced by the climate of opinion, which in turn is affected very considerably by the interests and attitudes, and therefore by the activities, of the political nation.[1]

Thus, he concluded, President Reagan and Mrs. Thatcher are merely in office, not in power. As events have unfolded since then, that conclusion may prove to have been premature, but his thesis was sound. A powerful minority, which cannot always guarantee the election of its own politicians, nonetheless can and does block the desires of the popular majority as expressed in national, state, and local elections.

A critical phrase in Bauer's description of the political nation is that it "dominates discussion" of political and governmental matters. More precisely, it sets the agenda, determining what is going to be discussed and then dominating the discussion. This is very subtle. One can go for years without realizing why things aren't changing. The answer is simply this: the issues and the viewpoints that many people would like to take up get little, if any, attention. Someone with an ax to grind is keeping the debate away from those viewpoints. Occasionally that someone lets such opinions be aired, but he determines the context and the manner in which they are presented.

There is a temptation to think that discovery of this situation points us only to what we Americans loosely call "the media," which has become a pejorative label to many of us of late. But the political nation or elite minority goes far beyond the media, the press, the journalists. The latter are merely a primary tool—the transmitters— of a much broader, more influential group.

No, the elite minority is bigger, more pervasive than the relatively small group of newsmen in the country. And even that statement makes it sound as though we're speaking of a highly coordinated and purposefully evil conspiracy. We're speaking of a gradually developing condition that has taken hold powerfully in the last seventy-five years, but never as effectively as in the last two decades. And its origins go back much further than that, if we consider the philosophers and theorists. Many, if not most, of its proponents are nice, decent people, albeit misled and misleading, in the view of a majority of Americans.

This elite minority touches much more than politics and government, too, although we are examining this area first because of the nature of our subject matter—the Reagan mystery.

Many people think of this political nation or elite minority as "the Establishment," the ones who are so strategically well-entrenched and holding so much power that they simply "run things." Others speak of "the system." This is the way it's always been done, they say, shrugging their shoulders, and the system sets the course.

A number of conservative intellectuals use the term *new class* in describing a major portion of this group, especially those who determine what's talked about in the various public forums. Jeane J. Kirkpatrick, social scientist and current ambassador at the United Nations, said, "They shape debate, determine agendas, define standards and propose and evaluate policies."[2]

The conservatives coined the phrase *new class* because the group has new, unprecedented power and larger ranks and because its members really form a class of values and goals that wields its influence through the producing and marketing of information.[3] It has been called the consciousness industry, the knowledge industry.

"What wealth is to the capitalist, what organization is to the old-style political boss, what manpower is to the trade unionists, words are to the new class,"[4] Mrs. Kirkpatrick said.

For the purpose of this book, I include the political nation, the elite minority, the new class sectors of society, and that which might be called the establishment or directors of the system. They are the ones who have been overriding the popular will in so many areas of life. And they are a minority.

Bauer referred to "progressive businessmen," a surprising inclusion at first glance, yet one of the most powerful segments of the political nation, although it is ironically cutting its own throat in a sense through its collaboration with those intent on the destruction of capitalism. Examination and reflection show that a significant portion of big business, including big banking, does indeed participate in the frequent manipulation of public policy away from majority public interest and toward its own global and national interests. Internationally, certainly, those interests tend to support a sort of liberal internationalism regardless of whether it harmonizes with the best interests of this nation.

Nationally, these same corporate entities, trying naively to be humanitarian and to serve "the public interest," support causes that subtly and steadily undermine the free enterprise system that allows the corporations to flourish. Although these big-business groups like to think warmly of themselves as political moderates, they do by their actions frequently ally themselves with leftists intent on thwarting the popular will.

Another odd inclusion in any listing of the elite minority is labor, although it must be quickly pointed out that no one includes the body of the labor movement, only a number of its leaders. Here the actions of those leaders, in ways that are contrary to the majority of the membership, seem to approach betrayal. Burton Yale Pines, a former correspondent and associate editor of *Time* magazine, who has devoted himself to political, economic, and social policy analysis, pinpointed the conflict:

> Ideologically inspired, too, is the opposition to traditionalists by a number of the nation's labor union leaders who stand considerably farther to the left than their rank and file. The AFL-CIO Executive Council, for example, in August 1979 called for nationalizing the country's oil industry. National Education Association leadership not only supports increasing federal involvement in nearly every sector of society (except defense) but opposes just about every traditionalist economic, social, political, and foreign policy position. Other labor proposals call for dissolving large corporations and penalizing firms which move plants or even shut down operations altogether. Some labor leaders, like William Winpisinger of the International Association of Machinists and Aerospace Workers, are avowedly socialist.[5]

Studies and voting patterns show that the majority of workers represented by members of this elite minority, this political nation, do not think like their leaders. How can this happen? The answer, obviously, is found in the power and deception of the knowledge industry.

Similar conditions are found in a significant part of the legal Establishment, although certainly not in all the ranks of individual lawyers struggling across the land to uphold the integrity of the law and law enforcement. Setting the pace, naturally, are the Supreme Court and the Federal circuit and district courts. Together with the self-proclaimed "public interest" groups, they have been striving successfully to shift power from elected bodies like Congress and state legislatures to unelected bodies like courts and agencies that are highly populated and influenced by the legal Establishment. This, of course, removes accountability to the popular will in elections and perpetuates minority views running contrary to majority opinion.

This long-running trend has thrown disproportionate power into the hands of groups like the American Civil Liberties Union, who argue in noble-sounding rhetoric that they are protecting the public interest. The truth is that they represent views greatly shaped by the counterculture of the sixties and seventies and are actually hostile to the desires of the popular majority. They show contempt for middle-class values, including those growing from American tradition or religious faith, and for free enterprise, hard work, and discipline.

Frequently functioning in close proximity to the legal elitism that pervades the system, whether it be political or social or religious, are those described as "influential and articulate groups in the civil service." They are the bureaucrats—not all of them, certainly, but a significant and well established number. They are the professionals, the unelected leaders who shape policy—the nudgers, the cajolers, the persistent activists who sincerely believe they know better than the elected office holders what is good for America. They know especially well how to play the game of politics. They know how Washington (or a particular state capital) works. They know how to play the press to the fullest.

The goal of these professionals is to promote their own agendas and their own careers and often their own ideologies. Because of their jobs and backgrounds, they tend to see solutions in terms of increased government. Often unwittingly, they target free enterprise as enemy number one.

Then there are the professional humanitarians, sometimes individuals but most often foundations or funds, whose roots oddly enough trace back to the free enterprise system that many of them now indirectly work to overturn. They provide havens for articulate, intelligent, and usually well-meaning individuals who are little concerned with the popular will but for "progress" and "liberation" and "advancement" according to their definitions. These foundations have massive financial and intellectual influence, much of it good, obviously, but often they are the instruments of ideological entrepreneurs who chart a course that is at odds with that desired by the vast majority.

This brings us, unhappily, to the centerpiece of the elite minority—"the media." With that tired phrase, we encompass the daily press and others who fall into the journalistic category, authors of longer works, entertainment writers and producers, critics, and so on. As we noted before, this category becomes the centerpiece of the political nation simply because it is its most powerful tool. Pines, who lays out the case clearly in his book, *Back to Basics,* describes part of the condition in this manner:

> Whatever the causes of the New Class world view, it does exist and, through New Class-dominated channels of information, bombards the public with anti-traditionalist arguments and sentiments. Nowhere is this more evident—or more threatening to traditionalist

gains—than in the news media, particularly the so-called national elite media comprised of television's three major networks, the nation's three leading newspapers—*The New York Times, The Washington Post,* and *The Wall Street Journal*—and two weekly newsmagazines, *Time* and *Newsweek.* By education, professional concerns, ambitions, income and peer reinforcement, the reporters and editors staffing these enterprises are mainly New Class (*The Wall Street Journal* less so than the others). They identify more with the values of Manhattan, Georgetown, and Beverly Hills than with those of Grundy Center, Iowa, or Lynchburg, Virginia. They almost all professionally inhabit the same one-fourth square mile of midtown Manhattan, dining and drinking in the same restaurants and bars, reading the same books, succumbing to the same fads and outraged by the same urban problems. Headquartered literally within a dozen blocks of elegant Rockefeller Center are *Time, Newsweek,* ABC, CBS, NBC, *The New York Times,* Associated Press, United Press International, *Fortune, Business Week, People,* and dozens of other media operations. Located there too and sharing the same values are the advertising and public relations firms which to a great extent shape America's tastes.

New Class values act as a prism distorting how this media elite receive and transmit data and ideas from and to Trans-Hudson America, that vast nation beyond Manhattan.[6]

The illustrations of the "prism" effect are numerous, and it's possible to take many cheap shots at it. Nonetheless, Pines' examples are reasonable and good, and those of us who have worked within those dozen Manhattan blocks can vouch for their accuracy. He notes that, after passing through the New Class value system, the leftists fighting in El Salvador's civil war become "guerrillas," while the rightists are described as "terrorists." This manipulation of language is extremely subtle, and I testify that a reporter or editor, pressed for time and space and the desire to communicate as best as he can, can slip into it and be engulfed before he's aware of it. But it occurs, and the results are devastating. Readers and viewers are manipulated. Those perceptive enough to recognize, through the senses and conscience, that skewing is somehow taking place will still be slow to discern what is happening. It is the selection of individual words and the juxtaposition of ideas that is subjecting them to values and orientations which are far from objective.

Pines cites another example that reveals the problem of selectivity:

It is a prism effect which also explains, apparently, the media elite's skewed coverage of the Reagan Administration's nomination of C. Everett Koop as U.S. Surgeon General. Reporting concentrated almost entirely on his outspoken opposition to abortion. Little was said about his professional qualifications for the post, such as his distinguished medical career—that he had longer tenure as surgeon-in-chief of a major hospital than anyone else in the U.S. and that he had been decorated by the French government for pioneering work in pediatric surgery.[7]

Much of the discussion has focused on the national media, especially that based in New York and Washington, for in many ways the publications and networks there set the pace for the rest of the nation. But the elitism problem extends beyond the borders of those two cities, to other power centers and to the entertainment industry.

General motion picture and television fare, for example, is filtered rather substantially through the same prism that news is. Particularly strong is the effect on national mores, especially those of young people and children. It works in several ways.

"The mass media," explained James Hitchcock, author and professor of history at St. Louis University, "also have the power to confer instant recognition." It's a devastating truth, the explanation for the unimaginable shift in moral and religious values since the mid-sixties. "No matter how seemingly 'neutral' the treatment," he said, "when certain ideas are given time and space in the media they acquire a respectability that increases with frequency. Then comes the point where previously taboo subjects become familiar and acceptable."

Hitchcock deplored "the media's pious claims" that they are not setting values but merely reflecting reality. "In fact," he declared, "the power of celebrity is used deliberately and selectively in order to effect changes in values."

He noted astutely that the media, especially the movie, stage, and television portions, are masters of ridicule, "the single most powerful weapon in any attempt to discredit accepted beliefs." As a result, Christians and others with traditional values, smothered by a savage barrage of satire, often find themselves adjusting their beliefs, or at least adjusting the ways they present them in public.

"Only people with an exceptionally strong commitment to their beliefs could withstand being depicted as ignorant buffoons," Hitchcock wrote. "Negative stereotypes were created, and people who believed in traditional values were kept busy avoiding being trapped in those stereotypes."

Hitchcock caused many newsmen and general writers to wince, I'm sure, with his hard-nosed insights on "the media's exploitation of traditional American sympathy for the underdog." One example will suffice:

> Judeo-Christian morality, although eroding for a long time and on the defensive almost everywhere in the Western world, is presented as a powerful, dominant, and even tyrannical system against which only a few brave souls make a heroic stand on behalf of freedom. Thus secularists of all kinds and those who deny traditional morality in words and behavior are treated as heroes by the media. Their stories are told over and over again in order to elicit sympathy and, finally, agreement.[8]

The facets of the condition seem unending. The media, itself elitist even within the elite minority, has wielded its enormous power for many years to overwhelm and override the will of the popular majority, in accordance with the will of the political nation, the liberal Establishment.

Naturally, there is a historical explanation for this fact. It requires that we see the various components we've outlined as essentially part and parcel of the same philosophy and value system. That philosophy and value system was passed on to all of them by one of their own—academia, or at least powerful portions of academia.

The educational community is the common denominator in all the categories we've examined. Especially do we find the major universities and their offspring in this role. They are centers of awesome, long-range power. Their effect on the elite minority is obvious and normal. Those who rise to influential leadership roles will be well educated and thoroughly exposed to the outstanding thinkers and scholars of the day. Those who rise to policy positions, no matter what part of the political nation they inhabit, will have been touched directly or indirectly by the leading political and social scientists of our time. And these latter educators, according to numerous surveys, are far to the left of the American mainstream, politically and socially. Great numbers of them are adamantly opposed to free enterprise and capitalism and in favor of an increasing role for government in virtually all matters.

The influence doesn't stop with the social sciences and politics, either. Thoughtful people, teachers of literature and the humanities, many of whom don't recognize their drift in values, shape attitudes that have consistently led to an increase in hedonism, a decline in morality, and an indulgence in selfish materialism.

One must avoid any tendencies toward anti-intellectualism in considering certain data formulated from surveys of Americans with varying degrees of education. For anti-intellectualism is as deplorable as the worship of intellectualism. Yet some of the survey results help us see the seriousness of what the elite minority has brought forth in the United States.

Driving to the heart of the issue was a pollster's question as to whether self-fulfillment was more important than providing economic security for a family. Fifteen percent of the high school graduates, those least exposed to the elite minority in education, answered yes; forty-five percent of college postgraduates answered yes. Self-indulgence has become rampant.

Asked about the importance of saving money, half of the high school graduates said it was not very important; two-thirds of the college postgraduates said it was not very important. Thrift has been devalued.

Is homosexuality wrong? High school graduates, 26 percent said no; college postgraduates, 57 percent said no.

Is adultery wrong? High school graduates, 26 percent said no; college postgraduates, 51 percent said no.

Is abortion on demand all right for married women? High school graduates, 43 percent said yes; college postgraduates, 70 percent said yes.

Is communism the worst form of government? High school graduates, 46 percent said no; college postgraduates, 75 percent said no.[9]

The litany goes on. But we needn't. The influence of educators, especially those of great prestige and access, is clear. But where did this deviation from traditional ideas, accompanied in many but not all cases by a leftward political drift, originate? How did academia, or this portion of it, slide into such a powerful position contrary to the mainstream?

Because of the religious nature of much of this book, it is important to acknowledge that the source of this shift, which produced an elite minority hostile to traditional values, was the Christian church itself. The church spawned, or allowed the spawning, of the deceit that evolved into secular humanism. And secular humanism is the philosophy (actually a religion) underlying the world view of the elite minority and much of the political nation. Thus, a major component of that Establishment, although no longer a very powerful component, comprises certain liberal clergymen and their various organizations. Their more conservative counterparts would consider them as the apostate church, not the Church of Jesus Christ, the Body of Christ.

These liberal groups, including numerous seminaries, appear to be bastions of anti-traditionalism regarding the United States, morality, business, family, and the like. A number of them have supported Marxist guerrillas in various parts of the world and opposed free enterprise in this country and elsewhere. Others have pressed for homosexual rights, abortion on demand, and unrestrained growth in the welfare state. And much of this has occurred contrary to the wishes of their church constituencies, certainly contrary to the expressed will of the American majority.

As to the fact of spawning the secular humanism that has undergirded the elite minority, one need only recall that education in this country, as elsewhere, was to a large extent the product of the church. The great universities of the land were originally grounded in the faith. They were designed to train young minds in godly ways for service to the nation and its citizens. They were founded by Christian people for Christian purposes. The Bible and faith in Christ were at the center of all.

What happened?

In the simplest terms, the problem began when a few church scholars ever so steadily de-emphasized the role of Jesus Christ in their world view. The trend eventually removed Christ's divinity, and the foundation of religion and its offspring, education, started to crumble. One truth after another fell victim to the move; absolutes vanished. The deification of man was underway. God soon became unnecessary, even unwanted. Agnostic neutrality gave way to atheistic opposition. Ultimately there was hostility.

Remember, this was a minority within the church. But that minority was articulate, aggressive, and persistent. Even strongholds of conservative theology felt the pressure. Man, made in the image of God, is a powerful creature, even when turning away from His Creator.

Ironically, Jesus and the writers of Scriptures warned that the greatest threat to Christianity would come from within the church. Error in doctrine—false teaching—would lead many into trouble, they said.[10]

Jesus Himself warned especially that His followers were to: "Take heed that no one leads you astray. For many will come in my name, saying, 'I am the Christ,' and they will lead many astray."[11] He told of "false prophets" who would "arise and lead many astray." Deception, He indicated, would be the weapon of His enemy.

So we see, as we survey the condition of education and its contributions to the elite minority—to secular humanism specifically—that the church or those moving under the guise of the church must share in the blame. For Paul spoke firmly to the church that there could be no other foundation for life than that which God Himself laid, "which is Jesus Christ."[12] Yet the church allowed false teachers to degrade and even remove the foundation, which holds everything together. It allowed man to be substituted.

That is the origin of the prevailing ethic—the religion—of much of the elite minority, the political nation. Today that ethic or religion is described as secular humanism. It sprang from the church, to education, to the media and its forerunners, and on into significant, highly educated, highly articulate channels of society.

"This shift," said Francis Schaeffer, "has been *away from* a world view that was at least vaguely Christian in people's memory (even if they were not individually Christian) *toward* something completely different—toward a world view based upon the idea that the final reality is impersonal matter or energy shaped into its present form by impersonal choice."[13]

It will help our considerations of the impact of these changes on the country and world in which we live today, the ones faced by Ronald Reagan as president, if we look at one of Schaeffer's descriptions of humanism:

> The humanist world view includes many thousands of adherents and today controls the consensus in society, much of the media, much of what is taught in our schools, and much of the arbitrary law being produced by the various departments of government.
>
> The term *humanism* used in this wider, more prevalent way means Man beginning from himself, with no knowledge except what he himself can discover and no standards outside of himself. In this view Man is the measure of all things, as the Enlightenment expressed it.[14]

Of course, it needs to be understood that, despite frequent indications to the contrary, humanism does not always instantly produce a sharp decline in an individual's morality. However, through the removal of absolutes and the substitution of man for God, it sets the stage for eventual decline and ultimate evil. As all will verify, not all humanists are evil, but simply in error, in varying degrees.

Furthermore, it needs to be understood that liberalism or even leftism are not to be equated with instant immorality or anti-Christianity. They merely set the stage, usually through the eventual glorification of the state above God and the individual. Neither is political conservatism to be equated with Christianity. They often can be far apart.

At the same time, it must be noted that humanism has shown itself as an ethic/religion that in the long term eventually produces leftism and a disastrous decline in historically proven values, although these two developments do not always occur at the same pace.

One is able to find a number of men and women in Washington today who understand the condition facing Reagan and its origins. This is significant. Until fairly recent years, one was hard put to find Christians or conservatives either bold or informed enough to articulate their cases in a manner competitive with that of their liberal, secular opponents.

Thomas W. Pauken, director of ACTION, the agency for volunteer service, spoke realistically, yet optimistically, about the situation facing the Reagan administration.

"You have what I call the popular majority," he said, "that's the average American. Reagan overwhelmingly was elected by the popular majority—the average man or woman. Then there is what I would call separately an intellectual majority—in the media, in the academic community, in all of those cultural areas—and the dominant ethic of the intellectual majority is at odds with the dominant ethic of the popular majority."

Leaning forward in his chair, hands on knees, fingertips occasionally touching, he pressed on: "I mean, if you look at the survey of George Washington University professors on 'Media and Business Elites,' and look at how they voted, they voted overwhelmingly for George McGovern in 1972. They voted overwhelmingly for Jimmy Carter and John Anderson against Ronald Reagan in 1980."

Of course, in both those cases the popular majority voted just the opposite in overwhelming numbers.

"So," Pauken said, "you have this conflict between people who basically control the intellectual machinery and thus try to elect people who have opinions like their own—'the best and the brightest are those who believe the way we do'—and consequently you have a situation where there's a tremendous amount of friction going on in this society."

But the Texan showed confidence in Reagan's abilities to handle the conflict. "I think the key is—I think Reagan, when he goes directly to the people, can get his message across. When it is filtered out by the media and distorted, or—that's the problem. The stories they select to cover and those they select to ignore have enormous consequences, which the average person doesn't really pick up on. This is a very difficult problem for him. In the long term, for men like Ronald Reagan to be able to govern, we're going to have to get a fair shake in the media and in the academic community."

Even on this point, he was correctly optimistic. Changes are occurring. "We now have, in my opinion, the intellectual talent that can compete," he said. "We didn't have it twenty years ago. When you look at the new columnists—George Will, Joe Sobran, Tom Bethel—the talent is enormous. But they don't have enough places to put them. A conservative, no matter how qualified he or she is, who goes to a CBS or an ABC or NBC, unless they already have a name like a George Will, they're not going to be selected in, and that's my argument."

He straightened in his chair, smiling ever so slightly. "There's no conspiracy, but it's just sort of this frame of reference that people have. I sat on the panel selecting White House Fellows in 1971 and I went around—I was associate director—and I went around to these panels and I saw how brilliant people who had the 'wrong' ideas— that is, they didn't go along with the liberal Establishment—somehow got selected out, and it really opened up to me how subjective this process can be."

Pauken also understood the origins of the "ethic" dominating the intellectual community. "I think it's humanism," he said, "secular liberalism. My argument goes that traditional Christianity, Protestantism, as the dominant religious force in our society became very rationalistic at a certain period of time and then after a while, the religious aspect got dropped. It's a little bit like, I make the argument— I happen to be a Catholic—there are some priests out there who have been priests for twenty or thirty years and, that's all they know, and they've got this institution, and some of them have lost their faith (lost their Christian and traditional Catholic belief) and yet they have the institution and they want to hold on to it. And you look at the National Council of Churches and some of the Protestant segments, as well as the U.S. Catholic Conference, and you wonder, 'What is the substance of their beliefs?' "

A brooding sadness covered his face for a few moments. The words were obviously difficult for him to speak, and it was clear he did not approach the matter lightly or judgmentally. "It's sort of, when men put God out of their lives, or deny—it's sort of, God disappears— whether agnosticism or atheism—"

Again, Pauken, who seemed to exemplify the attitudes of all those in the administration who were interviewed on the matter of the elite minority, was optimistic. He illustrated it with a recollection of a Soviet writer's image showing that if one paved the whole world over with concrete, some day a crack would appear in the concrete, and from that crack, a leaf of grass would break through. "And that's sort of what's happened," he said, "only the cracks are getting bigger. And I think in a somewhat analagous sense, in the United States, with the dominant ethic being secular, the counter-culture is a religious-oriented culture, and it's very attractive to people. The true individualist looks around at conformity in this society and, if he wants to truly run against the grain, he becomes a Christian and becomes someone looking at traditional American values as the direction this country ought to go."

He concluded: "We are already competing in terms of ideas, but it's transmission of ideas where we're not able to compete."

There is a temptation, as one reads some of the new writers exploring values and trends in American life or talks to the many, many serious-minded younger thinkers and activists positioned in key places in Washington, to think significant change in the political nation is imminent. It may be. But several things must be remembered. Primary among them is that coercion—the forerunner of tyranny—is no more tolerable from the right than it is from the left. Those holding traditionalist, moral, family values must remember that persecution, no matter how subtle, has no place among those values. The hate and suspicion, say, of what we now call McCarthyism will not produce desirable change, politically or otherwise.

If Jesus Christ is, as we noted earlier, the foundation of true life, we must remember it was He who said we were to love God with all our beings and love our neighbor as ourselves. He did not say the neighbor had to be in agreement with us on all things.

Although optimism does seem justified regarding a turnabout in the domination of secular humanism and the current ethic of the elite minority, it is helpful to remember that the problem goes deeper than conservative or liberal politics or even a return to certain traditional values. It goes to the essence of mankind—to spiritual issues. And it may prove easier to bring forth a traditionalist or conservative revival than a spiritual one. Indeed, we must examine the question: Is a spiritual renewal possible in the United States and the world?

★ ★ ★ ★ ★ ★ ★ ★ ★ ★ ★ ★ ★ *13* ★ ★ ★ ★ ★ ★ ★ ★ ★ ★ ★ ★ ★

The Call for Renewal

FOR YEARS REAGAN HAS been saying that the United States needs a spiritual revival if it is to overcome its problems. Such a call is woven through his speeches, letters, and conversations all the way back to his time as Governor of California. It was still being regularly proclaimed in the second half of his first term as president. Indeed, on more recent occasions, his language was modified enough to suggest he perceived such revival to be underway.

At a Governor's Prayer Breakfast in 1972, for example, he said: "I think our nation and the world need a spiritual revival as it has never been needed before . . . a simple answer . . . a profound and complete solution to all the trouble we face."

To Christian educators, to youngsters, to the pope—the message was the same: "The time has come to turn back to God and reassert our trust in Him for the healing of America."[1]

What did he mean when he spoke of healing? In a letter to a narcotics control commissioner in Brooklyn, he described a conversation with Pope Paul VI. "I told him of the so-called Jesus Movement in America and how so many young people had simply turned from drugs to a faith in Jesus. As you can imagine, he was not surprised, nor should we be, for He promised that He was our salvation."

Regarding rampant sexual permissiveness, Reagan wrote: "I don't believe the answer rests with government. No one can legislate morality. What we need is a spiritual awakening and return to the morals of a Christian society."

He pursued a similar theme on hedonism and humanism, replying to a questioner with these words: "I am deeply concerned with the wave of hedonism—the humanist philosophy so prevalent today—and believe this nation must have a spiritual rebirth, a rededication to the moral precepts which guided us for so much of our past, and we must have such a rebirth very soon."[2]

In a television interview during his 1980 campaign, Reagan was asked if he saw cause for hope of a reversal of "moral pollution."

"Oh, yes," he replied, consistently the optimist. "It isn't too easy to see now, but I believe the tide has turned. I think that the hunger [for spiritual renewal] I mentioned earlier has become evident. I think the contrast of [the young people's] attitude today with a few years ago reveals this hunger. These problems won't be solved by some sudden sweeping over the land of a warning or something. It is going to come from within the people themselves. I think they are already feeling it."[3]

In the same interview he spoke about insights he had picked up during the days and nights of criss-crossing the land seeking re-election. "There is one thing about campaigning," he said. "We talk about how hard it is, but when you go out across the country and meet the people, you can't help but pray and remind God of that passage in 2 Chronicles [about healing the land], because the people of this country are not beyond redemption. They are good people and I believe this nation has a destiny yet unfulfilled."[4]

Although his letters and conversation on spiritual renewal often dealt on an individual level, Reagan continually made clear that he was also speaking of the nation as a whole. He was especially pointed in a statement issued in connection with the nation's bicentennial celebration:

> In this bicentennial year, we are daily reminded that our strength and our greatness grew from a national commitment to God and country. Those institutions of freedom which became famous world-wide were forged in the fires of spiritual belief; yet today many of these institutions are in jeopardy.
>
> The time has come to turn back to God and reassert our trust in Him for the healing of America. This means that all of us who acknowledge a belief in our Judeo-Christian heritage must reaffirm that belief and join forces to reclaim those great principles embodied in that Judeo-Christian tradition and in ancient Scripture. Without such a joining of forces, the materialistic quantity of life in our country may increase for a time, but the quality of life will continue to decrease.
>
> As a Christian, I commit myself to do my share in this joint venture.
>
> Our country is in need of and ready for a spiritual renewal. *Such*

a renewal is based on spiritual reconciliation—man with God, and then man with man. [Italics added.]

A bicentennial celebration is only important if we can learn from its history. One lesson should be that as a nation it's "In God We Trust."

America was ready, he felt. By early 1983, he was more and more using the present tense as his optimism rose. "There *is,*" he declared, "a great spiritual awakening in America—a renewal of the traditional values that have been the bedrock of America's goodness and greatness."[5]

He reported that a survey by a Washington-based research group had concluded that Americans were "far more religious" than the people of other nations. "Ninety-five percent of those surveyed expressed a belief in God," he said, "and a huge majority believed the Ten Commandments had real meaning in their lives."

Another study, he asserted, had shown "overwhelming" majority disapproval of adultery, teen-age sex, pornography, abortion, and hard drugs and a simultaneous "deep reverence" for family ties and religious belief.

Most mass communicators virtually ignored Reagan's hopes for spiritual renewal. Those who gave it much notice frequently were sarcastic. Hugh Sidey of *Time* was typical: "In the distance the president could see that same 'great spiritual awakening in America' that has been coming as long as preachers have preached."[6]

A Christian who has witnessed and participated in the remarkable renewal of the last twenty years in many countries, including the United States, bristles at such remarks. Yet he really shouldn't. For this very real revival, as widespread as it has been, has not made the kind of public impact that would be noticed by the average journalist. It has operated largely at an individual level, touching a number of groups and mainline denominations, but not *overtly* altering the course of society.

While acknowledging that, however, one must hasten to add that had it not been for the renewal, the condition of the country and the world would almost certainly be much worse than it is. It's impossible to prove, of course. The same holds true for the renewal of the late forties. Most of us who were unbelievers at that time were not aware that any such thing took place. This again forces us to remember Saint Paul's teaching that the unspiritual do not even recognize spiritual things.[7] But that renewal may have held the country together in a difficult postwar period, for the Holy Scripture says that in Christ "all things hold together."[8]

It is obvious in Reagan's speeches and conversations that he is speaking of a revival that will penetrate society at a deeper level than what we've experienced in this century. He's looking for a move of God that will affect morality, poverty, education, defense, arms control, commerce, everything. For he has come to recognize during the long and ongoing evolution of his Christian faith that man is helpless to help himself beyond a certain point. Should God withdraw from the world—which He will not—the planet would be doomed to deterioration and destruction despite man's best-intentioned activities.

No, Reagan is not looking for something "churchy." He's looking for something life-changing, something that touches the marketplace, the halls of government, the places where men crunch against one another. Although he speaks from a different and more optimistic perspective, he's actually closely aligned with the views of Aleksander I. Solzhenitsyn, who in Reagan's third year once again rattled the cages of his exile.

"The entire twentieth century is being sucked into the vortex of atheism and self-destruction," the Russian author declared in a widely covered address in London. "We can only reach with determination for the warm hand of God, which we have so rashly and self-confidently pushed away. . . . There is nothing else to cling to in the landslide."

Solzhenitsyn, whose soaring cries of anguish for the nations often prove so unsettling to Western political leaders, has seemed little able to alter the course of the steady slide into secular humanism that he deplores so vehemently. But his words seem momentarily to sting those lands still calling themselves Christian. One almost senses a brief hush of embarrassment when he speaks out, which is infrequently. His sufferings at the hands of the Soviets, as reflected in his best-selling books, seem to have elevated him to the level of guardian of the world conscience. Thus, significant numbers heard him once again warn of the secularism that he believed had been gaining force in the Western world since the Middle Ages with its "gradual sapping of strength from within."

They also heard him parallel a frequent statement by Reagan as to ultimate victory by God. "No matter how formidably communism bristles with tanks and rockets," he declared, "no matter what successes it attains in seizing the planet, it is doomed never to vanquish Christianity."

His appeal was for strength and courage—renewal—in the face of

worldwide communism. That, too, is the caliber of spiritual revival
sought by the President of the United States.

Is Reagan whistling in the dark with his perceptions of spiritual
renewal?

I asked Pat Boone, who travels throughout the country regularly,
if he thought the revival the president speaks of is actually happening.
He minced no words: "Yep."

Shirley, his wife, elaborated. "I believe we're seeing the glory of
God," she said. "I've spoken at the leadership conferences for women
in the Washington for Jesus Rally in 1980 . . . and I'll never forget
when we stood out on that mall and prayed and tore the strongholds
down, and I know that was a turning point. When all of us went
there and really started seeking God for our nation, and taking it
seriously, look what happened. And I know it's not going to stop
with what happened out on the mall."

She was speaking of the gathering in Washington in 1980 of half
a million Christian people from all over the country for the biggest
rally of its kind ever held in the United States. There was speechmaking,
preaching, singing, fasting, and prayer—a mass intercession of people
with God in behalf of the nation. It was perceived by reporters and
others as a conservative political rally, although its leadership firmly
denied it and no partisan politicking was evident. There were exhorta-
tions for individual and national repentance. And there were long
and loud prayers for God to direct the nation, to provide the political
and social leaders of His choice. All of this was especially impressive
at the height of the gathering when hundreds of thousands joined
together in mass prayers and supplications. Even many churchmen
who had been most skeptical about the propriety of such a rally were
moved by the unity of those hours.

Mrs. Boone, reflecting on the fact that the rally had not sought
the election of particular candidates but had instead asked that God
prevail, concluded: "We prayed them into those positions, and I'm
convinced beyond the shadow of a doubt that we're going to see mira-
cles."

She was not alone in her view of the 1980 rally and related events
as a milestone in modern American history. Bill Bright of Campus
Crusade, Demos Shakarian of the Full Gospel Business Men's Fellowship, Adrian Rogers of the Southern Baptist Church, Pat Robertson

of the Christian Broadcasting Network, and numerous pastors have voiced similar views. They speak not so much of numbers in an evangelistic sense as they do about the visible and invisible ramifications of having that many people united in reaching out to God for help.

With variations, they have spoken like Robertson: "We touched God that day—500,000 people—and we have seen many things change or begin to change since then." They speak particularly of the heightened awareness of and mounting opposition to abortion, pornography, homosexuality, and all symptoms of godlessness. They speak further of progress in the steady drive to allow children to pray in schools.

And many frankly point to the election of a Christian president who takes the lead in such matters. They report a sense of relief and optimism in many sections of the country, especially those areas so often overlooked by opinion leaders, areas not dominated by New York and Los Angeles. They speak of traces of a freshening spirit, sometimes almost imperceptible, stirring among the people.

Billy Graham was also optimistic about widespread revival in the United States and around the world. As he prepared for his crusade in Sacramento in the early autumn of 1983, he spoke in his hotel room of the duality of spiritual experience in the world.

"I always think of what the Lord said in His parable of the wheat and the tares," he explained, "that they both are growing at the same time. And it seems that we see an outburst of evil throughout the world on a scale that perhaps we've never known—through the drug culture, pornography, and all the other things that are happening, crime, and all the things we read in our headlines. But at the same time there's something else that doesn't make the headlines so much and that is the work and the power of the Holy Spirit, in which thousands of people throughout the world are turning to Christ."

But he suggested that even greater renewal was ahead and pointed to three major keys for bringing it forth—repentance, prayer, and obedience. "We must repent of our sins," he said, obviously speaking both individually and nationally, "and when we repent, God is going to hear our prayers."

A few moments later, he returned to the theme: "I think prayer is the key, and if we can get people burdened to pray—and obey—I think we have to bring that in, that we're going to have to *obey*."[9]

Evangelical pastors across the country, seemingly without exception according to responses to Graham's and Robertson's words, agreed in the expectation for unprecedented renewal.

Donn Moomaw, who is capable of speaking about deeply religious matters in quite unreligious language—much like the president—offered a good, hard-nosed opinion about the prospects for revival in America.

First, he pointed to the rapid rise of modern technology. "As it grows," he said, "it exceeds its ability to answer questions that are arising." As a result, he felt that people generally, and especially those involved in modern technology, were "by the process of elimination" turning elsewhere for more meaningful answers to their questions and their problems.

"This is good," he said, "because it can ultimately lead to a search for God." And, as any good pastor knows, anyone who honestly and sincerely searches for God will find Him.[10]

Moomaw noted that people, particularly many in Southern California, "seek money and they get money, but they don't have answers to life's problems." And that raises questions of "what now, what do we do now?" They're still faced with deep issues, the ones that eventually confront everyone—death, eternity, forgiveness of sins.

"Technology, which we're so very much swept up in, doesn't give answers to those questions," he said.

So the Presbyterian pastor believes a lot of people are saying, "Give us your best shot, church." The response to that, he said, "must be gutsy, it must be real, and it must be biblical, not philosophical." People don't need more philosophy; they need something that works.

"No one has discovered better answers than those given by Jesus of Nazareth," he declared.

Moomaw's great hope in all of this was that Christian people, those who have experienced God in their lives, "would demonstrate it in their businesses and in government and in their whole lives, not only in their talk."

He agreed with the president that there is evidence of a revival of sorts—"but what we must do is *live* as people of faith, not naively, but we must *live out* what we believe."

"People are itching," he said, "but they don't know where to scratch and they're looking for somebody to help them." The truths of the church are ancient, he pointed out, and they must be shown to be viable in a modern world.

With that, he concluded, the opportunities for revival are tremendous.

A forceful Christian scholar, Francis A. Schaeffer, agrees with Moomaw's call for changed lives among believers if a changed nation is to result. "We must not be satisfied with mere words," he said. "With the window open [for Christian action] we must try to roll back the results of the total world view which considers material-energy, shaped by chance, as the final reality. . . . Those who have the responsibility as Christians, as they live under Scripture, must not only take the necessary legal and political stands, but must practice all the possible Christian alternatives simultaneously with taking stands politically and legally. . . . Christians must not only speak and fight against these things, but must show there are Christian alternatives. . . . This is so, and especially so, even when it is extremely costly in money, time, and energy."[11]

Views such as Moomaw's and Schaeffer's—the call for living out one's faith in all aspects of life even at great cost and peril—are not new to the history of revivals. But they often are submerged in our day as we ebb and flow in a sort of super-spirituality that tends to ignore action to match faith. The Wesleyan Revival of the eighteenth century brought forth widespread social reforms in England, which we will focus on in the next chapter. The same thing occurred in the mid-nineteenth century, both in England and America.

However, with a few exceptions, the Christian renewal in this country in the last twenty or more years has not had the spillover into medical, hospital, prison, and ghetto matters to match those of previous centuries. It should be noted, though, that the current renewal appears to some to be poised for such breakthroughs, perhaps even into government.

Seven hundred years before the time of Christ, Isaiah the prophet was declaring that such breakthroughs go hand-in-hand with renewal.

> If you take away from the midst of you the yoke,
> the pointing of the finger, and speaking wickedness,
> if you pour yourself out for the hungry
> and satisfy the desire of the afflicted,
> then shall your light rise in the darkness
> and your gloom be as the noonday.
> And the Lord will guide you continually,
> and satisfy your desire with good things,
> and make your bones strong;
> and you shall be like a watered garden,
> like a spring of water,
> whose waters fail not.
> And your ancient ruins shall be rebuilt;
> you shall raise up the foundations of many generations;
> you shall be called the repairer of the breach,
> the restorer of streets to dwell in.[12]

In Isaiah's understanding, as in Moomaw's and Schaeffer's, the people's faith in God was to produce action. And that action was to include a proper observance of the Sabbath, an honoring of the day of the Lord, without neglecting justice and mercy. Then, and only then, would God make that marvelous nation "ride upon the heights of the earth."[13]

The point is: If renewal is to come to America, then faith in God is going to have to break out of the confines of the churches and into the marketplace. Reagan believes he sees that happening. A number of Christian leaders agree with him.

Pat Robertson, as the Reagan administration wound through its third year, was pointing his large and influential constituency toward the writings of the prophet Joel, probably dating to 800 B.C. or earlier. He believed he saw there a significant pattern for national revival.

Joel uses a monstrous locust invasion to set the stage for calling Judah and Jerusalem to repentance. Then he tells the leaders to call a fast, a solemn assembly, a gathering of the people. There is to be repentance and crying out to the Lord.[14] Robertson believes this may have occurred in this country at the Washington for Jesus Rally discussed by Shirley Boone.

Joel then foresees the Lord responding by sending prosperity upon the people—"grain, wine, and oil"—and driving away the invaders.[15] Robertson sees a certain fulfillment of this in recent days, especially among the believers who have been faithful even during hard times in giving themselves and their goods to the Lord's work.

This, according to the pattern, is to be followed and accompanied by an outpouring of the Holy Spirit[16]—great revival and great power—before the age moves into its final stages, including Armageddon, the return of the Lord Jesus, judgment, and the millennium.[17] In Robertson's view, we are on the brink of that huge work of the Holy Spirit and indeed may have moved into its fringes.

Another noted Christian leader, who has a good record for perceiving church renewal, is Ralph Mahoney, founder of World MAP (Missionary Assistance Plan). Because of his credibility, especially in world Pentecostal circles, his writings about the imminence of revival in North America drew considerable attention in 1982 and 1983.

"There is a sense in my spirit that we are on the verge of a new visitation of God right here in North America that is going to not only affect our continent, but others as well," he said.

Supporting his thesis with the Bible and events, Mahoney believed the most reliable "signboards" pointing to God's major acts in history are His people—Israel and the church—and the leadership of the two. They seem to parallel one another. First, he noted the recent conflicts in the Middle East and Israel's expansion of its effectual borders northward. He believed this was a prelude to "a fresh and new thing in the church," an expansion flowing into a major revival.

As for leadership changes, there were numerous possibilities. For example, Israel's top political leadership was aging—Prime Minister Menachem Begin had already resigned—and new figures were likely to rise quickly. Paralleling this in the church, particularly in the United States, several outstanding new leaders had moved into position in the last decade and could emerge as successors to those, like Billy Graham, for one, who had been so dominant for many years.

Such developments, which Mahoney indicated might already be happening, would in his view portend a move by God.

Pointing out that revival often doesn't look like revival in its first months and years, Mahoney believed that "the signs of the times" referred to by Jesus[18] were visible and that spiritual renewal, as desired by President Reagan, was just over the horizon.

"If what we anticipate happens, we are going to see a revival that brings so many converts into the churches they won't be able to cope with the explosive growth," he declared.[19]

Roy Rogers and Dale Evans, who are exposed to a wide cross section of Middle America, Christian and not, both felt the opportunities for national revival were excellent. "God is going to honor the people who are trying, and trying to do good, and trying to improve," Roy said.

"Yes," I responded, "but are you optimistic that people will start turning to the Lord?"

He didn't hesitate. "If we keep getting leaders of a high caliber who are not afraid to stand up there and talk about it." He made it clear that he believed President Reagan was of sufficiently high caliber and was indeed standing up and talking about commitment to the Lord and national renewal. "If they'll just give him another four years," he said, "I think he'll get our country back together."

Dale was equally optimistic. "This Christian heritage is the thing that Ronald Reagan is trying to make us remember, that our source of greatness in this country is God. It's not really weapons; it's not really science; it is God who gives it all."

She was correct. It seemed perfectly clear that any expectation for significant change in the very powerful "political nation" holding sway in the United States would depend on an act of God. Spiritual renewal, if widespread enough, could do it.

The grip of humanism and antigodliness is strong, but it can be broken—and rather quickly—by God. Large numbers of us who are Christians today were humanists first; many of us were anti-God. But the Holy Spirit can renew a mind. He can illuminate even the darkest corners.

We can, as a nation, return to the faith of our fathers. And as Schaeffer declared: "They knew they were building on the Supreme Being who was the Creator, the final reality. And they knew that without that foundation everything in the Declaration of Independence and all that followed would be sheer unadulterated nonsense. These were brilliant men who understood exactly what was involved."[20]

In the meantime, is Roy Rogers right? Can Reagan, while we wait upon God, hold the country together?

★ ★ ★ ★ ★ ★ ★ ★ ★ ★ ★ ★ *14* ★ ★ ★ ★ ★ ★ ★ ★ ★ ★ ★ ★

Can He Govern?

WE'VE EXAMINED THE MAN of faith. We've examined the man of conservative politics. We've seen him in the real world among real people. Now the question: Can he govern in a meaningful way and make a long-term difference?

I believe the answer is clearly yes. But a number of conditions must develop for the answer to become a resounding one.

For one thing, President Reagan must walk uprightly before the Lord. That was the condition set forth in the 1970 prophecy regarding his ascension to the presidency. It remains a condition if God is to prosper his service fully.

For another, the elite minority must little by little be overpowered and outperformed. Those with faith and traditional values must earn their way.

For another, spiritual renewal must come to the country. The advance of materialism and decadence has been great, even among those professing some degree of religious belief. Only such a move upon our very disparate people can produce the long-term unity that will be required.

The outlook for each of these conditions is favorable from Reagan's point of view, although certainly not conclusive. His challenge will be to project enough promise of fulfillment of them by election day, 6 November 1984, that his popular mandate of 1980 will be renewed. Opposition to that challenge will be powerful.

Even should he succeed, however, the conditions will remain. A full turnaround for the United States will not come overnight.

As for Reagan himself, there is no indication that at this point in his life he intends to back away from his commitment to Christ and His teachings or his commitment to traditional social and political values. All evidence at every level of observation points to the contrary. He seems to be growing stronger in his perception that, for individuals and for nations, there is only one way ultimately.

This came immediately clear during an interview in the Oval Office as a typically hectic Friday afternoon drew to a close and Reagan prepared to head off for some horseback riding and a weekend at Camp David. It was 14 October 1983, a few weeks after the Soviet downing of the Korean airliner and a few days before the terrorist bombing of the U.S. Marine barracks in Lebanon. The burdens of the presidency had seldom seemed heavier. Yet for a few minutes in the fading afternoon sunlight, the magical charm of his concentration upon a friendly chat with a single, relatively insignificant visitor proved to be even more real than writers had reported.

I asked him how he felt about his Presidency thus far, in terms of effecting the turnaround spoken of so often in his campaign and the early days of his administration.

He looked straight into my face, a slight smile on his lips, and he spoke softly at first. "What I have felt for a long time," he said, "is that the people in this country were hungry for what you might call a spiritual revival, a return to values, to things they really believed in and held dear. And I always remembered that Teddy Roosevelt said this office was a bully pulpit, and I decided that if it was possible for me to help in that revival, I wanted to do that."

With a short pause, he pressed on. "I feel very strongly that when you get down to the very tough questions, the tough problems, you have to ask yourself—not whether it's political or whether it gains votes—you have to ask yourself what to the best of my ability do I conceive as being right or wrong—best for the people—and make a decision that way."

A smile broke across his face and his eyes sparkled for an instant. "And I find you don't age as quickly if you do that." They were in essence the same words he had spoken to Harald Bredesen on that fall afternoon in Sacramento thirteen years earlier, the day the small group's prayer pointed toward the White House.

At the time of our interview, the President had not officially declared himself a candidate for reelection, although many campaign pieces were falling into shape. So asking about the future was tricky. He was willing to talk, but he was not about to fall for a loaded question.

I asked him how he would press forward to complete the turnaround that he desired for the country, assuming that he did not believe the job had been completed. "Would you do anything different, more intensely?" I asked.

He smiled at my awkwardness in trying to pose the question discreetly and then answered:

"If I had that opportunity—so far we've had to be dealing with immediate problems—we've had to be dealing with the recession, with the world the way it is, the trouble spots, where we're involved, and I believe involved because it is in our national interest to be involved. If there were more time, I would like to feel that we could then make some of these things that we've accomplished—the attempt to reduce the size of the government, and so forth—that we could then make them more permanent and install them so that they would be around for a while. And I think of them actually in terms of getting this government back—this isn't something new—of getting the government back to where it once was and where it should be.

"For example, I believe very strongly that one of the great secrets of our individual freedom is the fact that we were created uniquely in our world to be a federation of sovereign states. As a matter of fact, I remember in 1932, the Democratic platform upon which Franklin Delano Roosevelt ran at that time—one of his planks had to do with restoring to states and local communities the authority and autonomy that had been unjustly seized by the Federal government. And it also called for a reduction in the power and the cost and size of the Federal government.

"Well, our Federalism program is based on that same idea. Of course, that [Roosevelt] platform was never implemented, even though they won the election. And I was a Democrat at that time; I voted that way.

"But, yes, I think there are things that can be [done]—and I would like to see it completely permanent, of course—but that would put the government into a different basis and a different direction."

I asked him if he believed the institutions of government could be modified to the point, where, whether he was president or not, they could not be turned around quickly. Was he optimistic about his goals?

"Yes," he said, "I really am, because I'm optimistic about the people of this country. We started a thing called the Private [Sector] Initiative, and this was to persuade private groups—the private sector—to do many things that over recent years we've just taken for granted [that] only the government could or should do. And the response

has been unbelievable. All over this country. We have here now—
we have a permanent office here for the Private Initiative—the private
sector—this type of work. They have a computer with more than
three thousand programs in it that are being performed out in the
country some place, in communities and states, by private enterprise
groups, local government groups, from neighborhood groups on up,
to tremendous-size undertakings.

"To give you an example of that, one day in a ceremony out here
in the Rose Garden, a little nun here temporarily from overseas, where
she has a clinic—a medical base out there, in the undeveloped country—she whispered to me that her commissary—for helping the hungry
there—that they just were in desperate need of flour. And I whispered
back I would see what we could do. And I came in and I called
our Private Initiative office, and just told them about this situation.
They called back in an hour and said three thousand pounds of flour
were ready to aid her commissary."

Our conversation shifted to the international realm, and I asked
the president whether he was optimistic about dealing with the Soviet
Union in the future since relations between the two superpowers affect
most world affairs.

"Well," he began, "I think the tragedy of the [Korean] airplane
revealed to many people that some of the things I had been trying
to call to their attention were true—that you don't deal with them
as seeing them in a mirror image. But I also believe that they're very
practical about their own welfare. And I have an optimism based
on the fact, or the idea, that if we can show them—not appealing to
them that this is a nice thing to do—[but] show them that they can
actually be better off and that their own safety and their own living
standards and all could be benefited by a different approach than
they presently have—that peace could be very beneficial to them. And
I just believe that the practicalities are such that if we can make
them see some of these points, they might turn—not because they've
had a change of character—but [because] it's to their advantage to
do these things."

The westerner remained the optimist, convinced that all things were
possible, even peace and prosperity for a massive, pluralistic nation
and for a divided world. And once again, in the final minutes of
our conversation, he made plain the foundation of his optimism. During those awkward moments of closing an unusual interview with
an unusual political leader, I told about a young man at the Christian
Broadcasting Network. The man, a videotape operator, knowing I

was headed for the interview, had insisted that I inform Reagan that employees at the television network were praying for the president and the government in the manner prescribed by St. Paul regarding governing authorities.[1]

Reagan looked into my eyes and said softly, "Would you tell him thanks, because I happen to believe very firmly and deeply in intercessory prayer. And I think that I feel a strength because that is going on, and people are doing that, and I've been told by others. So would you give him my heartfelt thanks?"

I nodded, ready to depart. But the president continued. "And you might tell him a little anecdote from me. When I first became governor, it seemed the situation was pretty much like it was here at the Federal Government. It seemed as if every day when I sat down at my desk, there was somebody in front of me telling me that we had another problem. And it became an almost irresistible, physical urge of mine— I really mean this—to turn and look over my shoulder as if there were someone maybe I could turn to and say, 'Hey, we have a problem.' And then one day I just realized that I was turning in the wrong direction, and I started looking up instead of over my shoulder, and things immediately got better."

Reagan's difficulty in the weeks or months or years ahead will continue to be the expression of that faith despite a pluralistic society and despite the attitude of several of those working for him who honestly believe they are serving him best by muting his commitment. He will need extraordinary wisdom.

This will be part of the issue of letting Reagan be Reagan. He will have strong opposition purely on political grounds; colleagues will continue to fear the possibility of offending anyone who does not agree with Reagan's religious beliefs. These colleagues fail to perceive the mood of the land. Ordinary citizens are tired of wishy-washy stands. They're tired of people who talk but seem to say nothing. They frankly dislike people without convictions, even if they don't agree with every jot and tittle of those convictions.

America's recent history contains episodes that would curl the hair of anyone with the slightest religious belief (and recent polls declare unequivocally that religious interest and involvement are rising markedly in the United States). President Carter, for example, at a particularly appropriate moment talked with the President of South Korea about the possibilities of committing one's life to Christ. They were riding in the presidential limousine in Seoul and were overheard by State Department personnel accompanying them. According to a government official in a position to know about the incident, "these people just freaked out." To them, it was intolerable for the President of the United States to talk seriously and persuasively about God with another top political leader.

Although it may be difficult for the average citizen to understand how subordinates could cause trouble over such events, nonetheless they did and effectively imposed roadblocks to head off other extraordinary spiritual activities.

The effectiveness of the roadblocks was evident when President Carter attempted to respond to efforts aimed at getting him and the leader of another nation to meet to pray about world problems affecting their nations. Carter's letter, according to a knowledgeable administration source, was placed in his out box but was not delivered.

"How could they get away with that?" I asked.

"Because they were in concert with the State Department," the source replied.

Attempts to arrange for a number of world leaders to meet with other presidents, including Reagan, are also reported to have been made. "We have offers by foreign leaders—by those people who said they would like to be in a prayer process with the president," according to one informed government figure.

"Why haven't we jumped on that?" I asked.

"Well, because the staff around him are not receptive to that kind of thing, and it's been true for a period of time," he replied. "Carter had the same offer."

This is the sort of attitude Reagan will have to deal with if he is to fulfill his desire to make a meaningful change in the country. George Gallup reports a growing conviction in the United States that religion is the only answer to the problems of the world. For example, he said, Americans declare by a 2-1 ratio that they are more likely today than five years ago to say that religion can answer the problems of the world.[2] If that perception is correct, then presidential aides may be guilty of thwarting solutions if they persist in their attitudes.

Reagan himself will probably have to take the initiative to break out of the shell.

Donn Moomaw, concerned particularly about the president's own spiritual nurturing, felt Reagan may have to "take the risk" that attending public worship involves. He suggested experimentation on the part of the president, the Secret Service, and the press to develop some way for President and Mrs. Reagan to go to church. They would not necessarily have to go to the same church every Sunday, in Moomaw's view, and they would not have to disclose their plans in advance. "They should just go, quietly," he said. "The newspeople ought to lend him a hand on this and not try to cut in on it for their own purposes."

The president needs to be out among the people, the California clergyman said. Mutual encouragement and support would obviously result from such elbow-rubbing, and the Reagans would be refreshed simply by hearing biblical truths expounded, by praying with others, and by such profoundly simple acts as worshiping through singing.

As Reagan approached his fourth year in office, there were indications that steps were being taken to make such public worship possible.

At the White House, I inquired as to the possibilities of Reagan's one day meeting with two, three, or four people—preferably staffers but not necessarily so—to regularly pray and perhaps examine the Scriptures together. This would be in keeping with the small meetings going on throughout the government.

"Yes, I could see that happening," replied one presidential adviser. "I don't know if it will or not, but I could see that happening. I think it would be more likely to happen on a specific situation rather than just as a regular thing."

Another administration official familiar with procedures at the White House replied even more positively: "He would do it instantly. All he needs to do is get through his staff. And the person that protects him from that is Mike Deaver. If I were in Mike Deaver's spot, what I would do is mention it—he'd say yes, and he'd do it. It's just that it's not mentioned. He longs for this type of thing." (Efforts to meet with Deaver to discuss this were unfruitful.)

A minister acquainted with the Reagans and most of official Washington concurred. "If they would, any of them, ask the president to sit down and meet and just go through what it means to be a disciple of Christ—I know two or three people—he'd do it just like that."

He snapped his fingers for emphasis. "The problems of our day are not solved by a Democrat or a Republican or whatever. They're not; they're way beyond that." Having moved for many years among governmental leaders of every persuasion and background, he spoke with considerable authority. "We have to have a new type of man, a new type of leadership, a leadership . . . led by God. And, you know, the finest Christians cable the president and tell him how to lead—

and they say God spoke to them. And another group tells him just the opposite on the same day. And that's rampant when a man becomes known as a Christian. Well, what we should do, in my view, is get off that and pray—you know, a fundamental thing about a man in Christ is that he's led by the Holy Spirit. What we want is for the Holy Spirit to lead the president, and then we would have unbelievable solutions to the most difficult situations, which may not come to him until the very moment he needs to know."

He paused a moment and smiled fleetingly. "And that would give me tremendous confidence—that I knew the man was being led, not by Meese, not by Deaver, not by Clark, or not by the Congress, but by God. That's what we need in this country and in all the countries of the world."

Again, this man, who because of his work insisted that he remain unidentified, spoke with authority, having ministered in fifty-five third-world countries in the previous two years.

Probably the biggest obstacle to something of this nature occurring in Reagan's administration is his overwhelming fear of being perceived as "exploiting" his Christianity to impress people or to appear to be pious and holier-than-thou. This fear is deeply ingrained, along with a dislike for appearing to coerce others to follow his beliefs.

Timing and wisdom will be required. But the president must come to the full realization that a majority of America is now on his side in these matters. As one aide noted, "I think his way is more to reassure people, to get them thinking in really a new way, or to make them feel that what they always felt in their hearts is not wrong, and not to be embarrassed about it. And he must not do it in a way that is so shrill that it sets his tone up to be what is criticized—rather than what he says."

Many of Reagan's old and close friends were rooting for him in these matters. Pat Boone was typical. He went so far as to hope Reagan might some day, under the right circumstances, actually lead the nation in prayer, rather than merely calling for a moment of silent prayer as he did following his nomination.

"I don't know if Reagan ever would publicly lead the nation," he said. "I'd love to see him do it, because I think the President of the United States should voice the prayer. I think it would be great."

He paused, looked at his hands, and then added, "Reagan just might do that some day, and I will encourage it." He obviously meant to voice the possibility to his old friend at some appropriate moment. "But the thing is to respond to the president—our response ought to be to pray for him because he wouldn't be there if God hadn't put him there. That was true with Carter; it was true with Ford; it was true even with Nixon."

Boone's optimism that Reagan might one day be bold enough to lead the nation in prayer was shared by numerous aides and officials in Washington. "You just have to pray that God will put that together," said one at the White House.

As for the elite minority, there was evidence that even if it is not directly overpowered, it may one day be outmaneuvered. Actually both may happen.

In the face of considerable opposition, for example, the Reagan administration had set in motion more substantive change in its first three years than a superficial review might reveal, although the change was far from completed.

First, the administration had produced a widespread, perhaps even a nationwide, commitment to a strong national defense.

Second came a commitment to realistic dealings with potential adversaries, especially the Soviet Union. This commitment was swept with controversy after the Soviet air force shot down a Korean civilian airliner on 1 September 1983, killing 269 people. A high number of conservatives felt the administration did not deal forcefully enough with Moscow over the incident, notwithstanding the small number of realistic options. There was reason to believe, however, that Reagan, a patient bargainer who understood the Soviets long before the airliner tragedy, intended to stand firm and that his measures would be long term.

A third significant modification taking place under Reagan's leadership was a reinforced commitment to America's allies, who had gone through several years of uncertainty. Personal rapport with other leaders was a key factor in this change.

Fourth was a redirected commitment to arms-control negotiations.

Fifth was the ongoing commitment to peace in the Middle East, although this commitment had produced debatable strategy and less than successful results in that churning part of the world.

Domestically, many of the changes were still short of midstream, although the commitment had been clearly made, seemingly with nationwide approval, to try to reduce dependence on the Federal government and shift focus to the states and the private sector. This had produced a significant amount of deregulation and redirection of activity within numerous agencies, although transfer of activities to states had not kept pace and was still to be worked out.

Long-term success for Reagan depends on his administration's ability to change institutions to such a degree, so to speak, that the turnaround can take hold and not be easily turned back, either by default or manipulation.

I asked the presidential counselor, Ed Meese, about progress in this direction. "The special interest groups, the media—which is of a liberal orientation—the people who think there should be a strong central government and are not worried about the states and local government—they're all there," he said. "But I would think that just as you had a change in direction, say in the thirties—and since then you've had accelerated, unrestricted growth toward bigger and bigger government—I think that now the expansive growth of the central government probably has been pretty much contained, at least for a considerable period of time. This is due to the public consensus that has developed, although you still have some pressure along these other lines, as I said."

I asked him how the Reagan administration expected to sustain and expand any of its gains against the elite minority, the political nation. "Basically by getting the facts out and by acquainting the people with what the situation is, to start with, and then with what the president is doing and why he's doing it," he replied. "It's a matter of getting the word out and getting the word across. That's the most difficult problem."

Tom Pauken of ACTION probably offered the most direct and promising advice for overcoming that "difficult problem" of getting the word out through the media, which truly is Reagan's most trying challenge.

"I think Ronald Reagan has shown that a man of conservative principles and Christian convictions can govern the United States," he said, "particularly when he is able to carry his message directly to the American people, because I think the American people are looking for men and women in politics who believe in some principles rather than the pragmatic types who can float from one position to another. I think the American people sense that this hasn't worked very well and that those people are not the kind of leaders we need in these very difficult times."

He slowed his rapid-fire delivery for just an instant. "Now, in terms of the long-range situation, I think it is more important perhaps now than previously for people of Christian and conservative convictions to begin to involve themselves more in the media, in the academic community, in the world of letters and TV and film and radio, because that community is dominated by folks who by and large are secular and liberal. And given their own biases, they tend to select out [reject] opinions, viewpoints, people who disagree or dissent from that ethic."

Interlocking three fingers of each hand, he raised them and touched his pursed lips with the forefingers, then smiled ever so briefly. "So I think if we can move more in that direction, because the intellectual talent is out there on our side now—we just need to get them placed in the institutions—then the conservative philosophy could well be the dominant political philosophy for the next generation in the United States. And I think it needs to be if this country is going to turn itself around."

He concluded: "Ronald Reagan as a president, for the first time, rather than simply going along with the direction we were heading in, has started to turn things around. But we can't expect that *he* can do *everything*—or ask too much of the man. He is at least setting us on the right course, but we've got a long way to get to the place where we want to go."

Ben Elliott, the head presidential speechwriter, generally agreed with Pauken's thesis but emphasized a crucial dimension: the great need for patience and perseverance if the elite minority, particularly the media, is to be affected. I asked him about the pervasiveness of the political nation, the establishment of old.

"Yeah, it's a tremendous problem," he said. "It's the greatest challenge we face. All the powers-that-be are mobilized in practically every instance to oppose what is the right, although difficult, course to take. And therefore it takes someone with incredible skill and vision and courage—a willingness to ignore the petty-type atmosphere that pervades this town—and have the faith to not see only the mountain but to look beyond it, because if you keep going, you're going to end up there."

Leaning back from his desk in the old executive office building, Elliott, formerly of CBS, clasped his hands behind his head and continued:

"There are some things that are beginning to show. Even though people stand up and nitpick against him on fifteen different points, he is able to convince enough people that the thrust of what he's saying has merit, that we must move in this new direction—and they [the political nation] have not been able to turn that off. In education, they said, 'Well, Reagan was wrong,' but Ronald Reagan was right and most people would agree, even though he's being criticized [by the Establishment] because he cut education spending."

Looking directly at me and smiling for an instant, he interjected: "CBN made the comparison on 'The 700 Club' that while spending was going up, SAT scores were plummeting, and the fact of the matter is that people who are criticizing Reagan are the same people once again who did nothing while this problem was developing. The same with the economy—they did nothing. The same with the military— they did nothing. And then Reagan is the guy who comes in and says, 'We must change it.' Now, he's only beginning. But things are already beginning to percolate so we think that there is an attitude change that is happening in the country, and those attitudes will lead to concrete action that people will support."

I asked him about the problem of getting through to the people.

"He has to be realistic and honest [when he speaks to them], because, first of all, the problems are enormous and we can't arouse—we can't blow up expectations to the point where people will hold the promises against you. They can say, 'Well, you obviously failed.' You can only say, 'It's better now than it was before, and it's going to be a little bit better tomorrow.' "

I interrupted him. "But how do you transmit that? Some say the transmission of the message is the hard part."

"That's true," he replied, "because there are so few people in the Washington Establishment who honestly believe in their hearts that what he's doing is the right thing to do, so the president goes out and makes a statement. And then if a hundred other people come in and say, 'You're wrong'—what we have is one voice against a hundred voices. So in terms of numbers, we lose.

"I think there has to be a certain acknowledgment that what we're up against is so tremendous in terms of their power and their organization and their influence, in so many different areas of our society, that you can't come in and just stand up and scream from the housetops without being considered some kind of a nut. Ronald Reagan is not that kind of a president. He wants to reassure people and then be able gently to take them along—because that's more his way of doing things."

It was clear to all that the competition between the people of religious and traditional values and the people of the political nation would be rugged and would require endurance. But the competition was underway, and it was steadily progressing toward evenness.

In terms of spiritual renewal, the task was even more monumental. But fortunately the burden of it rests with God and therefore becomes quite possible.

Britain's John Henry Overton, the historian of the eighteenth century church, understood the importance of renewal to the success of a leader. "It is extremely difficult," he wrote, "for any man to rise above the spirit of his age. He who can do so is a spiritual hero."[3]

Now Reagan may not turn out to be a spiritual hero, but it seems abundantly clear that without a sweeping revival exceeding anything we've known, no leader can be expected to bring about a lasting healing of the problems in our land. Neither will he stand much chance of reversing permanently the slide toward anarchy and ultimate dictatorship of the right or the left.

Fortunately, the marks of revival are showing in this country, as we've seen. Indeed, they are showing more with each month. In September 1983, Gallup said a survey "clearly indicates a rising tide of interest and involvement in religion among all levels of society."

He added: "Nearly six in ten Americans say they are more interested in religious and spiritual matters than they were five years ago." According to his testing, 56 percent of Americans say they are more reliant upon God than they were five years ago.

The survey found the following significant point hanging in the balance: "About one-third of Americans [35 percent] say they form their political opinions based on religious beliefs to a greater extent than five years ago, but nearly as many [27 percent] say 'to a lesser extent,' while the balance [21 percent] say about the same."[4] The question is, how will that balance swing?

The findings, which may prove to be the most significant in the history of the nation, brought forth the following musings by Pat Robertson before the staff of CBN: "There is a season for everything. . . . And people now sense that a season for revival is here. . . . They are now spiritual-minded and interested. . . . Yes, they need more understanding, more teaching. . . . They're not focused. . . . But the season is here."

Personally, the conditions that Gallup, Robertson, and others perceived stirred memories of the winter of 1971 when I alerted editors at the *New York Times* in writing that America was in the early-to-middle stages of a spiritual renewal that would make a deep impact upon the country. I was certain that the bubblings of the Jesus Movement and the charismatic renewal would reach a full boil. I recommended knowledgeable, in-depth reporting on the trend, stressing the need for reporters experienced in renewal to undertake the work. Adequate coverage could not be provided by someone only peripherally or educationally acquainted with life-changing Christianity. Unhappily, meaningful reporting was not forthcoming, although the *Times,* like most of the media, dabbled in coverage, failing to penetrate the surface. When the renewal breaks upon the land, they will be virtually unprepared to understand what has happened. When it touches the government, education, banking, big business, they will be scrambling to catch up.

The media's inadequacies in the matter are understandable. The institutional church's unpreparedness is not. Yet it is generally unprepared. It, too, will have to scramble to catch up. It will need more preachers, teachers, Bibles, buildings, counselors—everything.

An inkling of what Reagan needs to accomplish his heart's desire in bringing forth a lasting turnaround in this country can be gained from a glimpse at late-eighteenth-century England provided by Garth Lean, former political columnist, now a best-selling British author:

> The awakening so improbably initiated by the quiet Oxford don [John Wesley], together with his brother Charles and George Whitefield, swept through the lower—and increasingly the middle—classes. In the fifty years preceding Wilberforce's conversion, John Wesley alone had travelled 225,000 miles up and down the kingdom, mostly on horseback, and preached more than 50,000 sermons in halls, at fairs, in military camps, on any open space where he could gain a hearing. The 700 full-time lay preachers working with him in the 1780's (almost all "unlearned men" in the eyes of the bishops) were scarcely less active. For them "no weather was too inclement, no road too boggy, no ford too swollen, no community too degraded, no privation too severe." One travelled not less than 100,000 miles on one horse. Another, his horse worn out, walked 1,200 miles in one winter. All were persecuted as were the Wesleys themselves: some being killed by mobs, others carried off by press gangs, many having their houses burnt over them, while the clergy and local big-wigs often egged on the attackers. But tens of thousands of lives had been changed by a faith which, in Overton's words, "made selfish men self-denying, the discontented happy, the worldling spiritually minded, the drunkard sober, the sexual chaste, the liar truthful, the thief honest, the proud humble, the godless godly, the thriftless thrifty."
>
> As the century proceeded, the awakening worked its way upward in society and George Whitefield in particular interested some and converted a few among the aristocracy. . . .

Such was the situation with which Wilberforce was faced as he set out to "reform the manners [morals and ethics] of England." It was a formidable task for a man of twenty-seven, even though he was the Prime Minister's best friend, the Member [of Parliament] for Yorkshire and one of the ablest speakers in the House of Commons.[5]

From that came the greatest reforms England, and perhaps any other country, has ever known. It took many years and extraordinarily hard, intelligent, disciplined work by William Wilberforce and a marvelous group of Christian politicians. But they eventually brought about the end of the slave trade in England, penal reform, child-labor reform, vast improvements in institutions of every kind, and a measurable change in ethics and morals among the population as a whole.

This is the sort of possibility that appears to have been thrust before the United States if the great revival that preachers have been seeking for decades finally reaches the scale being forecast by the likes of Robertson, Graham, Mahoney, Gallup, and Reagan.

Wilberforce and his colleagues, a remarkable gathering of leaders, recognized a fact that one will have to grasp if he wants to see a national move toward righteousness and justice. As he waits for the inner change in men, women, and children to occur in significant numbers, he must work hard to hold the ground and maintain an atmosphere in which the inner change can most easily occur. To do this, Wilberforce and his cohort pressed forward on three fronts, more or less in this order:

First, establish respect for the law. Maintain order. Preserve the peace.

Second, make goodness fashionable. Convince by example that goodness, if only for the sake of goodness, makes for a happier life than evil does. Encourage good instincts. Discourage—even outlaw—the exercise of some bad ones.

Third, use every opportunity to show that the source of all good is God Himself and that it is possible to live in harmony and communion with Him. Break through the misunderstanding that merely "doing good," without considering the purposes of God, will lead to long-term happiness and prosperity, individually or nationally.

Anyone desiring a turnaround in America for long-term good, whether it be Reagan or someone else in future years, would do well to heed this two-hundred-year-old example. It worked then. Because human nature remains the same, it will work now.

Reagan has several immediate problems with which he must deal that directly or indirectly touch upon any attempt to move in these directions. His greatest need is for an understanding as to how to move positively on those problems without falling into the game plan of his critics and opponents.

For example, conventional news reporting in 1983 hammered away at the "gender gap," Reagan's allegedly poor standing with women. His difficulty lay in getting off the defensive and communicating positively and convincingly his desire to elevate the real position of women in society. He was constantly forced to dissipate his energies defending his conclusion that the Equal Rights Amendment was a short-sighted and unsatisfactory way to help women rather than voicing his own affirmative approaches.

In the early spring of 1983, months before the quadrennial rampage for election, the Republican National Committee and certain White House advisers were wringing their hands over the women problem. They were on the defensive. This rubbed off onto the president, and the real Reagan, one who actually wanted to do something meaningful for women, was sidetracked.

To begin with, women need to be recognized beyond secured rights. They need to be recognized, not as combatants against men, but as a vital part of society that must be free to sustain and increase that vitality. One person who knows his thinking on these matters pointed to Reagan's awareness that there is "great confusion in many women's hearts and minds . . . a great hunger for identity—to know who they really are." Self-esteem is often at the core of the confusion. Women "really need to hear a positive, affirming voice that establishes how important they are."

Reagan needed to get off the defensive, refrain from repeating his critics' criticisms, and provide that "positive, affirming voice." He had improved the legal climate for women, he had improved the economic climate, he had improved the political climate. He must press forward on the social climate. Legislation or constitutional amendments will not do it for him. Positive, confident, moral leadership will help; God alone can provide the rest—changed hearts and renewed minds.

Another example of the problems with which Reagan needed to deal immediately concerned his standing with black Americans. Conventional political wisdom led to fear in this area. But, again, Reagan's proper course needed to be a positive one. He must not let his opponents dictate the script, if he is to succeed as the leader of all the people.

If, as many friends believed, he had reached that point where his inner eyes no longer saw black or white or brown or yellow when he looked at a man or a woman, then he must transmit that. He must make goodness believable and fashionable.

Economically, he had another immediate problem. The key phrase was "budget deficits." To preserve earlier accomplishments, he needed to find a way out of that quagmire. His basic philosophy had moved things in the right direction, but if he was to maintain order—respect for the law, in a sense—he and his associates in every branch of government needed to complete the task.

Again, positive, ethical, moral leadership—not defensiveness—was the way. Merely cutting social spending would not complete the job. Merely raising or lowering taxes could not generate enough, regardless of one's economic bent. Creative action, thoroughly explained to the people step by step, to eliminate the national debt, quickly, perhaps through a combination of one-stroke actions, was the type of action the American people were waiting for. They somehow sensed that the nation contained the creative power to execute something like that. Somehow, they thought, there must also be a creative way to be strong militarily without bankrupting the nation. Somehow, they felt deep down, we have the intelligence under God to solve this problem.

And so it goes. The challenges are there, but so are the responses. They're not easy, but they *are* relatively simple.

What are we to conclude?

In chapter 2 we first posed the question of whether a person of Reagan's persuasion could govern this most unique of nations with lasting effects. He's a believer who wants to obey God. He's a conservative sincerely believing in traditional values. In this chapter of conclusions, we're still posing the same question.

The answer, we've said, is a conditional yes.

The Nixon administration, so promising at moments, faltered with the first condition—the need to walk uprightly.

The Carter administration, preceded by so much hope, failed in the second condition, succumbing to the power of the political nation, the elite minority, and wallowing in ambiguity.

In each case, the third condition was not forthcoming: spiritual renewal did not fully break forth but continued to smoulder beneath the surface of society.

What about the Reagan administration? It now has experience, a track record from which to launch itself. The potential for success has not been greater in our century.

★ ★ ★ ★ ★ ★ ★ ★ ★ ★ ★ ★ *15* ★ ★ ★ ★ ★ ★ ★ ★ ★ ★ ★ ★ ★

The Documents—An Appendix

RONALD REAGAN, AS WE'VE SEEN, walked and talked with new vigor and boldness after his administration had turned the corner into its third year. The reasons were not complicated. First, he was more comfortable in his job. Second, some of those who impeded efforts "to let Reagan be Reagan" were overridden. Third, the issues demanded firmness, especially in spiritual and moral terms.

Quite simply, the president became more like the candidate he presented in 1980. His convictions once again surfaced.

The event that first caused heads to turn came at the convention of the National Religious Broadcasters in Washington. Long-time broadcasters hailed it as the best speech any president had delivered to their body. Their enthusiastic reception heartened the president noticeably. He had rediscovered that there were reasonable people out in the land who felt the way he did and who yearned to be encouraged.

Within weeks, he followed through with an even more detailed sketch of his aspirations. This came before the National Association of Evangelicals meeting in Orlando. This was the speech that so visibly aroused vocal segments of the political nation, who for spiritual reasons that they themselves don't understand are often blinded by rage over public displays of religious conviction, especially by a governmental leader.

The tempo of the administration picked up markedly in the days, weeks, and months ahead. The president stood his ground regarding convictions, and became perhaps even more aggressive as the 1984 re-election campaign eased into sight. Even so, many conservatives felt he wasn't being tough enough, and the liberals were seething.

183

Being president of all the people was no easy matter, as thirty-nine other chief executives had learned. If anything, the job was becoming more difficult.

Since most parts of the country are not served by media that provide primary documents such as presidential speeches, it seemed like a good idea to reprint transcripts of the N.R.B. and the N.A.E. speeches, along with a third chosen more or less at random, to show how the trend developed. The third was made to a relatively small gathering marking Captive Nations Week. Weather forced the group to move from its scheduled meeting in the Rose Garden to a small auditorium in the old executive office building.

The first speech includes the remarks of the President at the Annual Convention of National Religious Broadcasters, Sheraton Washington Hotel, Washington, D.C., 31 January 1983. The second script is the speech given by President Reagan at the 41st Annual Convention of the National Association of Evangelicals at the Sheraton Twin Towers Hotel, Orlando, Florida, on 8 March 1983. The third and last speech was given by the President during the Captive Nations Week Observance Ceremony, Executive Office Building, The White House, Washington, D.C., 19 July 1983.

You all have an expression among you that, first of all, you confess to being poor audiences for others. I haven't found it so. But you also have an expression about preaching to the choir. I don't know just exactly what my address—how that fits under that today. But what a wonderful sight you are.

In a few days I'll be celebrating another birthday which, according to some in the press, puts me on a par with Moses. That doesn't really bother me because every year when I come here, when I look out at your warm and caring faces, I get a very special feeling, like being born again.

There is something else I've been noticing. In a time when recession has gripped our land, your industry, religious broadcasting, has enjoyed phenomenal growth. Now, there may be some who are frightened by your success, but I'm not one of them. As far as I'm concerned, the growth of religious broadcasting is one of the most heartening signs in America today.

When we realize that every penny of that growth is being funded voluntarily by citizens of every stripe, we see an important truth. It's something that I have been speaking of for quite some time—that the American people are hungry for your message because they are hungry for a spiritual revival in this country. When Americans reach out for values of faith, family, and caring for the needy, they're saying, "We want the Word of God. We want to face the future with the Bible."

Facing the future with the Bible—that's a perfect theme for your convention. You might be happy to hear that I have some "good news" of my own. Thursday morning, at the National Prayer Breakfast, I will sign a proclamation making 1983 the Year of the Bible.

We're blessed to have its words of strength, comfort, and truth. I'm accused of being simplistic at times with some of the problems that confront us. I've often wondered—within the covers of that single book are all the answers to all the problems that face us today if we'd only look there. "The grass withereth, the flower fadeth: but the word of our God shall stand forever." I hope Americans will read and study the Bible in 1983. It's my firm belief that the enduring values, as I say, presented in its pages have a great meaning for each of us and for our nation. The Bible can touch our hearts, order our minds, refresh our souls.

Now, I realize it's fashionable, in some circles, to believe that no one in government should order or encourage others to read the Bible. Encourage—I shouldn't have said order. We're told that will violate the constitutional separation of church and state established by the founding fathers in the First Amendment.

Well, it might interest those critics to know that, none other than the father of our country, George Washington, kissed the Bible at his inauguration. And he also said words to the effect that there could be no real morality in a society without religion.

John Adams called it "the best book in the world." And Ben Franklin said: "The longer I live, the more convincing proofs I see of this truth, that God governs in the affairs of men . . . without His concurring aid, we shall succeed in this political building no better than the builders of Babel; we shall be divided by our little, partial, local interests, our projects will be confounded, and we ourselves shall become a reproach, a by-word down to future ages."

So, when I hear the First Amendment used as a reason to keep the traditional moral values away from policymaking, I'm shocked. The First Amendment was not written to protect people and their laws from religious values. It was written to protect those values from government tyranny.

I've always believed that this blessed land was set apart in a special way, that some divine plan placed this great continent here between the two oceans to be found by people from every corner of the earth—people who had a special love for freedom and the courage to uproot themselves, leave their homeland and friends to come to a strange land. And when coming here, they created something new in all the history of mankind: a country where man is not beholden to government, government is beholden to man.

I happen to believe that one way to promote, indeed to preserve, those traditional values we share is by permitting our children to begin their days the same way the members of the United States Congress do—with prayer. The public expression of our faith in God through prayer is fundamental— as a part of our American heritage and a privilege which should not be excluded from our schools.

No one must be forced or pressured to take part in any religious exercise. But neither should the freest country on earth ever have permitted God to be expelled from the classroom. When the Supreme Court ruled that school prayer was unconstitutional almost twenty-one years ago, I believe it ruled wrong. And when a lower court recently stopped Lubbock, Texas, high school students from even holding voluntary prayer meetings on the campus before or after class, it ruled wrong, too.

Our only hope for tomorrow is in the faces of our children. And we know Jesus said: "Suffer the little children to come unto me, and forbid them not for of such is the kingdom of God." Last year, we tried to pass an amendment that would allow communities to determine for themselves whether voluntary prayer should be permitted in their public schools. And we failed. But I want you to know something: I am determined to bring that amendment back again, and again, and again, and again until—

We were frustrated on two other fronts last year. There are five million American children attending private schools today because of emphasis on religious values and educational standards. Their families, most of whom earn less than $25,000 a year, pay private tuition and they also pay their full share of taxes to fund the public schools. We think they're entitled to relief. So, I want you to know that shortly, we'll be sending legislation back up to the Hill and we will begin the struggle all over again to secure tuition tax credits for deserving families.

There is another struggle we must wage to redress a great national wrong.

We must go forward with unity of purpose and will. And let us come together, Christians and Jews, let us pray together, march, lobby, and mobilize every force we have, so that we can end the tragic taking of unborn children's lives. Who among us can imagine the excruciating pain the unborn must feel as their lives are snuffed away? And we know medically they do feel pain.

I'm glad that a Respect Human Life Bill has already been introduced in Congress by Representative Henry Hyde. Not only does this bill strengthen and expand restrictions on abortions financed by tax dollars, it also addresses the problem of infanticide. It makes clear the right of all children, including those who are born handicapped, to food and appropriate medical treatment after birth and it has the full support of this administration.

I know that many well-intentioned, sincerely motivated people believe that government intervention violates a woman's right of choice. And they would be right if there were any proof that the unborn are not living human beings. Medical evidence indicates to the contrary and, if that were not enough, how do we explain the survival of babies who are born prematurely, some very prematurely?

We once believed that the heart didn't start beating until the fifth month. But as medical instrumentation has improved, we've learned the heart was beating long before that.

Doesn't the constitutional protection of life, liberty, and the pursuit of happiness extend to the unborn unless it can be proven beyond a shadow of a doubt that life does not exist in the unborn?

And I believe the burden of proof is on those who would make that point.

I read in the *Washington Post* about a young woman named Victoria. She's with child, and she said: "In this society we save whales, we save timber wolves and bald eagles and Coke bottles. Yet everyone wanted me to throw away my baby." Well, Victoria's story has a happy ending. Her baby will be born.

Victoria has received assistance from a Christian couple, and from Save-A-Life, a new Dallas group run by Jim McKee, a concerned citizen who thinks it's important to provide constructive alternatives to abortion. There's hope for America; she remains powerful and a powerful force for good; and it's thanks to the conviction and commitment of people like those who are helping Victoria. They're living the meaning of the two great commandments: "Thou shalt love the Lord thy God with all thy heart, and with all thy soul, and with all thy might"; and "Thou shalt love thy neighbor as thyself."

Each year, government bureaucracies spend billions for problems related to drugs and alcoholism and disease. Has anyone stopped to consider that we might come closer to balancing the budget if all of us simply tried to live up to the Ten Commandments and the Golden Rule?

That's what's happening with CBN, and the "700 Club's" "Operation Blessing." They've given nearly $2.5 million dollars to more than 8,500 churches and this money is then matched by local churches. The result has been fantastic: More than 100,000 needy families helped, either through direct or in-kind contributions ranging from food and clothing to education, dental care, and housework.

The PTL TV network is carrying out "A Master Plan for People that Love," opening centers all across the country to provide food, clothing, furniture, and job bank centers at no cost. Don't listen to those cynics—some of them here in the capital—who would run our country down. America's heart is strong, and its heart is good.

You know, I mentioned drugs a moment ago. And I hope you'll forgive me if I digress just long enough—because I don't often get the chance to say this publicly—how proud I am of Nancy, and the job she's doing helping to fight drug addiction.

I know that each of you is contributing, in your own way, to rebuilding America, and I thank you. As broadcasters, you have unique opportunities. And all of us, as Protestants, Catholics, and Jews, have a special responsibility to remember our fellow believers who are being persecuted in other lands. We're all children of Abraham. We're children of the same God.

You might be interested to know about a few of the changes that we're making at the Voice of America. Our transmissions of Christian and Jewish broadcasts are being expanded and improved. This year, for the first time in history, the Voice of America broadcast a religious service worldwide, Christmas Eve at the National Presbyterian Church in Washington, D.C.

Now, these broadcasts are not popular with governments of totalitarian powers. But make no mistake, we have a duty to broadcast. Alexander Herzen, the Russian writer, warned, "To shrink from saying a word in defense of the oppressed is as bad as any crime." Well, I pledge to you that America will stand up, speak out, and defend the values we share. To those who would crush religious freedom, our message is plain: "You may jail your believers. You may close their churches, confiscate their Bibles, and harrass their rabbis and priests, but you will never destroy the love of God and freedom that burns in their hearts. They will triumph over you."

Malcolm Muggeridge, the brilliant English commentator, has written, "The most important happening in the world today is the resurgence of Christianity in the Soviet Union, demonstrating that the whole effort sustained over sixty years to brainwash the Russian people into accepting materialism has been a fiasco."

Think of it—the most awesome, military machine in history, but it is no match for that one, single man, hero, strong yet tender, Prince of Peace. His name alone, Jesus, can lift our hearts, soothe our sorrows, heal our wounds and drive away our fears. He gave us love and forgiveness. He taught us truth and left us hope. In the Book of John is the promise that we all go by. It tells us that "For God so loved the world that He gave His only begotten Son, that whosoever believeth in Him should not perish, but have everlasting life."

With His message, with your conviction and commitment, we can still move mountains. We can work to reach our dreams and to make America a shining city on a hill. Before I say goodbye, I wanted to leave with you these words from an old Netherlands folk song, because they made me think of our meeting here today. "We gather together to ask the Lord's blessing./

We all do extol Thee, Thou leader triumphant/ And pray that Thou still our defender wilt be./ Let Thy congregation escape tribulation./ Thy name be ever praised! Oh Lord, make us free!" To which I would only add a line from another song, "America, America, God shed His grace on thee."

Those of you in the National Association of Evangelicals are known for your spiritual and humanitarian work. And I would be especially remiss if I didn't discharge right now one personal debt of gratitude.

Thank you for your prayers. Nancy and I have felt their presence many times in many ways. And believe me, for us they've made all the difference.

The other day in the East Room of the White House at a meeting there, someone asked me whether I was aware of all the people out there who were praying for the president and I had to say, "Yes, I am, and I've felt it. I believe in intercessionary (sic) prayer." But I couldn't help but say to that questioner after he'd asked the question that—or at least say to them that if sometimes when he was praying he got a busy signal it was just me in there ahead of him.

I think I understand how Abraham Lincoln felt when he said, "I have been driven many times to my knees by the overwhelming conviction that I had nowhere else to go."

From the joy and the good feeling of this conference, I go to a political reception. Now, I don't know why, but that bit of scheduling reminds me of a story which I'll share with you.

An evangelical minister and a politician arrived at heaven's gate one day together. And Saint Peter, after doing all the necessary formalities, took them in hand to show them where their quarters would be. And he took them to a small single room with a bed, a chair and a table and said this was for the clergyman.

The politician was a little worried about what might be in store for him. And he couldn't believe it when Saint Peter stopped in front of a beautiful mansion with lovely grounds and many servants and told him that these would be his quarters. And he couldn't help but ask, "But wait—there's something wrong—how do I get this mansion while that good and holy man only gets a single room?"

And Saint Peter said, "You have to understand how things are up here. We've got thousands and thousands of clergy. You're the first politician who ever made it."

But I don't want to contribute to a stereotype.

So I tell you there are a great many God-fearing, dedicated, noble men and women in public life, present company included. And yes, we need your help to keep us ever mindful of the ideals and the principles that brought us into the public arena in the first place. The basis of those ideas and principles is a commitment to freedom and personal liberty that, itself, is grounded in the much deeper realization that freedom prospers only where the blessings of God are avidly sought and humbly accepted.

The American experiment in democracy rests on this insight. Its discovery was the great triumph of our founding fathers, voiced by William Penn when he said: "If we will not be governed by God, we must be governed by tyrants."

Explaining the inalienable rights of men, Jefferson said, "The God who gave us life gave us liberty at the same time." And it was George Washington who said that "of all the dispositions and habits which lead to political prosperity, religion and morality are indispensable supports."

And finally, that shrewdest of all observers of American democracy, Alexis de Tocqueville, put it eloquently after he had gone on a search for the secret of America's greatness and genius: "Not until I went into the churches of America and heard her pulpits aflame with righteousness did I understand the greatness and the genius of America. America is good. And if America ever ceases to be good, America will cease to be great."

Well, I am pleased to be here today with you who are keeping America great by keeping her good. Only through your work and prayers and those of millions of others can we hope to survive this perilous century and keep alive this experiment in liberty, this last, best hope of man.

I want you to know that this administration is motivated by a political philosophy that sees the greatness of America in you, her people, and in your families, churches, neighborhoods, communities—the institutions that foster and nourish values like concern for others and respect for the rule of law under God.

Now, I don't have to tell you that this puts us in opposition to, or at least out of step with, a prevailing attitude of many who have turned to a modern-day secularism, discarding the tried and time-tested values upon which our value system is based. No matter how well intentioned, their value system is radically different from that of most Americans. And while they proclaim that they are freeing us from superstitions of the past, they have taken upon themselves the job of superintending us by government rule and regulation. Sometimes their voices are louder than ours, but they are not yet a majority.

An example of that vocal superiority is evident in a controversy now going on in Washington. And since I'm involved, I've been waiting to hear from the parents of young America. How far are they willing to go in giving to government their prerogatives as parents?

Let me state the case as briefly and simply as I can. An organization of citizens sincerely motivated and deeply concerned about the increase in illegitimate births and abortions involving girls well below the age of consent some time ago established a nationwide network of clinics to offer help to these girls and hopefully alleviate this situation.

Now, again, let me say, I do not fault their intent. However, in their well-intentioned effort, these clinics have decided to provide advice and birth control drugs and devices to underage girls without the knowledge of their parents.

For some years now, the federal government has helped with funds to subsidize these clinics. In providing for this, the Congress declared that every effort would be made to maximize parental participation. Nevertheless, the drugs and devices are prescribed without getting parental consent or giving notification after they've done so. Girls termed "sexually active"—and that has replaced the word "promiscuous"—are given this help in order to prevent illegitimate birth or abortion.

We have ordered clinics receiving federal funds to notify the parents such help has been given. One of the nation's leading newspapers has created the term "squeal rule" in editorializing against us for doing this and we're being criticized for violating the privacy of young people. A judge has recently granted an injunction against an enforcement of our rule.

I've watched TV panel shows discuss this issue, seen columnists pontificating on our error, but no one seems to mention morality as playing a part in the subject of sex.

Is all of Judeo-Christian tradition wrong? Are we to believe that something so sacred can be looked upon as a purely physical thing with no potential for emotional and psychological harm? And isn't it the parents' right to give counsel and advice to keep their children from making mistakes that may affect their entire lives?

Many of us in government would like to know what parents think about this intrusion in their family by government. We're going to fight in the courts. The rights of parents and the rights of family take precedence over those of Washington-based bureaucrats and social engineers.

But the fight against parental notification is really only one example of many attempts to water down traditional values and even abrogate the original terms of American democracy. Freedom prospers when religion is vibrant and the rule of law under God is acknowledged. When our founding fathers passed the First Amendment they sought to protect churches from government interference. They never intended to construct a wall of hostility between government and the concept of religious belief itself.

The evidence of this permeates our history and our government. The Declaration of Independence mentions the Supreme Being no less than four times. "In God We Trust" is engraved on our coinage. The Supreme Court opens its proceedings with a religious invocation. And the members of Congress open their sessions with a prayer. I just happen to believe the school children of the United States are entitled to the same privileges as Supreme Court justices and congressmen.

Last year, I sent the Congress a constitutional amendment to restore prayer to public schools. Already this session there's growing bipartisan support for the amendment and I am calling on the Congress to act speedily to pass it and to let our children pray.

Perhaps some of you read recently about the Lubbock school case where a judge actually ruled that it was unconstitutional for a school district to give equal treatment to religious and nonreligious student groups, even when the group meetings were being held during the students' own time. The First Amendment never intended to require government to discriminate against religious speech.

Senators Jeremiah Denton and Mark Hatfield have proposed legislation in the Congress on the whole question of prohibiting discrimination against religious forms of student speech. Such legislation could go far to restore freedom of religious speech for public school students. And I hope the Congress considers these bills quickly. And with your help, I think it's possible we could also get the constitutional amendment through the Congress this year.

More than a decade ago, a Supreme Court decision literally wiped off the books of fifty states statutes protecting the rights of unborn children. Abortion-on-demand now takes the lives of up to one-and-one-half million unborn children a year. Human life legislation ending this tragedy will someday pass the Congress and you and I must never rest until it does. Unless and until it can be proven that the unborn child is not a living entity, then its right to life, liberty, and the pursuit of happiness must be protected.

You may remember that when abortion-on-demand began, many of you warned that the practice would lead to a decline in respect for human life, that the philosophical premises would be used to justify other attacks on the sacredness of human life, infanticide or mercy killing. Tragically enough, those warnings proved all too true: only last year a court permitted the death by starvation of a handicapped infant.

I have directed the Health and Human Services Department to make clear to every health care facility in the United States that the Rehabilitation Act of 1973 protects all handicapped persons against discrimination based on handicaps, including infants. And we have taken the further step of requiring that each and every recipient of federal funds who provides health care services to infants must post and keep posted in a conspicuous place a notice stating that "discriminatory failure to feed and care for handicapped infants in this facility is prohibited by federal law." It also lists a twenty-four-hour, toll-free number so that nurses and others may report violations in time to save the infant's life.

In addition, recent legislation introduced in the Congress by Representative Henry Hyde of Illinois not only increases restrictions on publicly financed abortions, it also addresses this whole problem of infanticide. I urge the Congress to begin hearings and to adopt legislation that will protect the right of life to all children, including the disabled or handicapped.

Now I'm sure that you must get discouraged at times, but you've done better than you know, perhaps. There is a great spiritual awakening in America—a renewal of the traditional values that have been the bedrock of America's goodness and greatness. One recent survey by a Washington-based research council concluded that Americans were far more religious than the people of other nations; 95 percent of those surveyed expressed a belief in God and a huge majority believed the Ten Commandments had real meaning in their lives.

And another study has found that an overwhelming majority of Americans disapprove of adultery, teen-age sex, pornography, abortion, and hard drugs. And this same study showed a deep reverence for the importance of family ties and religious beliefs.

I think the items that we've discussed here today must be a key part of the nation's political agenda. For the first time the Congress is openly and seriously debating and dealing with the prayer and abortion issues—and that's enormous progress right there. I repeat: America is in the midst of a spiritual awakening and a moral renewal and with your biblical keynote I say today, "Yes, let justice roll on like a river, righteousness like a never failing stream."

Now, obviously, much of this new political and social consensus that I have talked about is based on a positive view of American history, one that takes pride in our country's accomplishments and record. But we must never forget that no government schemes are going to perfect man. We know that living in this world means dealing with what philosophers would call the phenomenology of evil or, as theologians would put it, the doctrine of sin.

There is sin and evil in the world. And we are enjoined by Scripture and the Lord Jesus to oppose it with all our might. Our nation, too, has a legacy of evil with which it must deal. The glory of this land has been its capacity for transcending the moral evils of our past.

For example, the long struggle of minority citizens for equal rights, once a source of disunity and civil war, is now a point of pride for all Americans. We must never go back. There is no room for racism, anti-Semitism, or other forms of ethnic and racial hatred in this country.

I know that you have been horrified, as have I, by the resurgence of some hate groups preaching bigotry and prejudice. Use the mighty voice of your pulpits and the powerful standing of your churches to denounce and isolate these hate groups in our midst. The commandment given us is clear and simple: "Thou shalt love thy neighbour as thyself."

But whatever sad episodes exist in our past, any objective observer must hold a positive view of American history, a history that has been the story of hopes fulfilled and dreams made into reality. Especially in this century, America has kept alight the torch of freedom, not just for ourselves, but for millions of others around the world.

And this brings me to my final point today. During my first press conference as president, in answer to a direct question, I pointed out that, as good Marxists-Leninists, the Soviet leaders have openly and publicly declared that the only morality they recognize is that which will further their cause, which is world revolution.

I think I should point out, I was only quoting Lenin, their guiding spirit who said in 1920 that they repudiate all morality that proceeds from super-natural ideas—that is their name for religion—or ideas that are outside class conceptions. Morality is entirely subordinate to the interests of class war. And everything is moral that is necessary for the annihilation of the old, exploiting social order and for uniting the proletariat.

Well, I think the refusal of many influential people to accept this elementary fact of Soviet doctrine illustrates an historical reluctance to see totalitarian powers for what they are. We saw this phenomenon in the 1930s. We see it too often today. This does not mean we should isolate ourselves and refuse to seek an understanding with them.

I intend to do everything I can to persuade them of our peaceful intent, to remind them that it was the West that refused to use its nuclear monopoly in the forties and fifties for territorial gain and which now proposes 50 percent cuts in strategic ballistic missiles and the elimination of an entire class of land-based intermediate-range nuclear missiles.

At the same time, however, they must be made to understand we will never compromise our principles and standards. We will never give away our freedom. We will never abandon our belief in God. And we will never stop searching for a genuine peace, but we can assure none of these things America stands for through the so-called nuclear freeze solutions proposed by some.

The truth is that a freeze now would be a very dangerous fraud, for that is merely the illusion of peace. The reality is that we must find peace through strength.

I would agree to a freeze if only we could freeze the Soviets' global desires. A freeze at current levels of weapons would remove any incentive for the Soviets to negotiate seriously in Geneva, and virtually end our chances to achieve the major arms reductions which we have proposed. Instead, they would achieve their objectives through the freeze.

A freeze would reward the Soviet Union for its enormous and unparalleled military buildup. It would prevent the essential and long overdue modernization of United States and allied defenses and would leave our aging forces increasingly vulnerable. And an honest freeze would require extensive prior negotiations on the systems and numbers to be limited and on the measures to ensure effective verification and compliance. And the kind of a freeze that has been suggested would be virtually impossible to verify. Such a major effort would divert us completely from our current negotiations on achieving substantial reductions.

A number of years ago, I heard a young father, a very prominent young man in the entertainment world, addressing a tremendous gathering in California. It was during the time of the Cold War, and communism and our own way of life were very much on people's minds. And he was speaking to that subject.

And suddenly I heard him saying, "I love my little girls more than anything. . . ." And I said to myself, "Oh, no, don't. You can't—don't say that." But I had underestimated him. He went on: "I would rather see my little girls die now, still believing in God, than have them grow up under communism and one day die no longer believing in God."

There were thousands of young people in that audience. They came to their feet with shouts of joy. They had instantly recognized the profound truth in what he had said with regard to the physical and the soul and what was truly important.

Yes, let us pray for the salvation of all of those who live in that totalitarian darkness—pray that they will discover the joy of knowing God. But until they do, let us be aware that while they preach the supremacy of the state, declare its omnipotence over individual man, and predict its eventual domination of all peoples on the earth—*they* are the focus of evil in the modern world.

It was C. S. Lewis who, in his unforgettable *Screwtape Letters,* wrote: "The greatest evil is not done now in those sordid 'dens of crime' that Dickens loved to paint. It is not even done in concentration camps and labor camps. In those we see its final result. But it is conceived and ordered (moved, seconded, carried, and minuted) in clear, carpeted, warmed, and well-lighted offices, by quiet men with white collars and cut fingernails and smooth-shaven cheeks who do not need to raise their voices."

Because these "quiet men" do not "raise their voices," because they sometimes speak in soothing tones of brotherhood and peace, because, like other dictators before them, they're always making "their final territorial demand," some would have us accept them at their word and accommodate ourselves to their aggressive impulses. But, if history teaches anything, it teaches that simple-minded appeasement or wishful thinking about our adversaries is folly. It means the betrayal of our past, the squandering of our freedom.

So I urge you to speak out against those who would place the United States in a position of military and moral inferiority. You know, I've always believed that old Screwtape reserved his best efforts for those of you in the church. So, in your discussions of the nuclear freeze proposals, I urge you to beware the temptation of pride—the temptation of blithely declaring yourselves above it all—and label both sides equally at fault, to ignore the facts of history and the aggressive impulses of an evil empire, to simply call the arms race a giant misunderstanding and thereby remove yourself from the struggle between right and wrong and good and evil.

I ask you to resist the attempts of those who would have you withhold your support for our efforts, this administration's efforts, to keep America strong and free, while we negotiate real and verifiable reductions in the world's nuclear arsenals and one day, with God's help, their total elimination.

While America's military strength is important, let me add here that I have always maintained that the struggle now going on for the world will never be decided by bombs or rockets, by armies or military might. The real crisis we face today is a spiritual one; at root, it is a test of moral will and faith.

Whittaker Chambers, the man whose own religious conversion made him a witness to one of the terrible traumas of our time, the Hiss-Chambers case, wrote that the crisis of the Western world exists to the degree in which the West is indifferent to God, the degree to which it collaborates in communism's attempt to make man stand alone without God. And then he said, "For Marxism-Leninism is actually the second oldest faith first proclaimed in the Garden of Eden with the words of temptation, 'Ye shall be as gods.'"

"The Western world can answer this challenge," he wrote, "but only provided that its faith in God and the freedom He enjoins is as great as communism's faith in man."

I believe we shall rise to the challenge. I believe that communism is another sad, bizarre chapter in human history whose last pages even now are being written. I believe this because the source of our strength in the quest for human freedom is not material but spiritual. And because it knows no limitation, it must terrify and ultimately triumph over those who would enslave their fellow man. For in the words of Isaiah: "He giveth power to the faint; and to them that have no might he increaseth strength. But they that wait upon the Lord shall renew their strength; they shall mount up with wings as eagles; they shall run and not be weary."

Yes, change your world. One of our founding fathers, Thomas Paine, said, "We have it within our power to begin the world over again." We can do it doing together what no one church could do by itself. God bless you and thank you very much.

Today we come to show solidarity with our brothers and sisters who are captives, not because of crimes that they have committed but because of crimes committed against them by dictators and tyrants.

We met here last month with a group of Baltic Americans honoring Baltic Freedom Day. And I said that we gathered to draw attention to the plight of the Baltic people and to affirm to the world that we do not recognize their subjugation as a permanent condition.

Today, we speak to all in Eastern Europe who are separated from neighbors and loved ones by an ugly iron curtain, and to every person trapped in tyranny, whether in the Ukraine, Hungary, Czechoslovakia, Cuba, or Vietnam, we send our love and support and tell them they are not alone. Your struggle is our struggle. Your dream is our dream. And someday you, too, will be free.

As Pope John Paul told his beloved Poles: "We are blessed by divine heritage; we are children of God; and we *cannot* be slaves."

The prophet Isaiah admonished the world: "Bind up the brokenhearted, to proclaim liberty to the captives." Some twenty-five centuries later, philosophers would declare that "the cause of freedom is the cause of God." We Americans understand the truth of these words. We were born a nation under God, sought out by people who trusted in Him to work His will in their daily lives, so America would be a land of fairness, morality, justice, and compassion.

Many governments oppress their people and abuse human rights. We must oppose this injustice. But only one so-called revolution puts itself above God, insists on total control over people's lives, and is driven by the desire to seize more and more lands. As we mark this twenty-fifth observance of Captive Nations Week, I have one question for those rulers: If communism is the wave of the future, why do you still need walls to keep people in, and armies of secret police to keep them quiet?

Democracy may not be perfect. But the brave people who risk death for freedom are not fleeing from democracy. They're fleeing to democracy from communism.

Two visions of the world remain locked in dispute. The first believes all men are created equal by a loving God who has blessed us with freedom. Abraham Lincoln spoke for us: "No man," he said, "is good enough to govern another, without the other's consent." The second vision believes that religion is opium for the masses. It believes that eternal principles like truth, liberty, and democracy have no meaning beyond the whim of the state. And Lenin spoke for them: "It is true that liberty is precious," he said, "so precious that it must be rationed."

Well, I'll take Lincoln's vision over Lenin's—and so will citizens of the world, if they're given free choice. Now some believe we must muffle our voices for the cause of peace. I disagree. Peace is made—or broken—with deeds, not words. No country has done more or will strive harder for peace than the United States. And I will personally embrace any meaningful action by the Soviet Union to help us create a more peaceful, safe, and secure world. I welcome the Soviet pledge of cooperation at the Madrid Review Conference on security and cooperation in Europe. With every ounce of my being, I pray the day will come when nuclear weapons no longer exist anywhere on earth.

And as long as I am president, we will work day-in, day-out to achieve mutual and verifiable reductions in strategic weapons.

When Congress approved the MX Peacekeeper program last May, America demonstrated its bipartisan consensus to implement the recommendations of the Scowcroft Commission. This bipartisan step marked progress toward genuine arms reductions. In the next few days, the Congress will vote on the question of supreme importance: Do we continue forward, or do we turn back from the Scowcroft Commission's recommendations? In terms of speaking to the world with one bipartisan voice, of standing up for U.S. vital interests, and of strengthening America's agenda for peace, no question matters more for this country in 1983.

Rather than seek temporary, partisan advantage, let us work together for the future of mankind. We must not waver in our quest for genuine peace and cooperation. We must keep our military strong to deter aggression. And we will never shrink from speaking the truth.

Ask yourselves: Was it our words that destroyed peace in Afghanistan, or was it Soviet aggression? Is peace served by sealing our lips while millions are tortured or killed in Vietnam and Cambodia? Or should we not speak out to demand those crimes be stopped? It's not provocative to warn that, once a communist revolution occurs, citizens are not permitted free elections, a free press, free trade unions, free speech, or freedom to worship, own property or travel as they please.

Many military regimes have evolved into democracies. But no communist regime has ever become a democracy, provided freedom, or given its people economic prosperity.

We will speak the truth. Alexander Herzen, the Russian writer, warned: "To shrink from saying a word in defense of the oppressed is as bad as any crime." That's why we want improved and expanded broadcasts over Voice of America, Radio Free Europe and Radio Liberty. And that's why we want, and the Cuban people need, Radio Marti. Now many of you here have known the suffering I've described. You are the conscience of the free world. And I appeal to you to make your voices heard. Tell them: "You may jail your people. You may seize their goods. You may ban their unions. You may bully their rabbis and dissidents. You may forbid the name *Jesus* to pass their lips, but you will never destroy the love of God and freedom that burns in their hearts. They will triumph over you."

Help us warn the American people that, for the first time in memory, we face real dangers on our own borders, that we must protect the safety and security of our people. We must not permit outsiders to threaten the United States. We must not permit dictators to ram communism down the throats of one Central American country after another.

We've seen construction in Cuba of a naval base from which Soviet nuclear submarines can operate. We see Soviet capacity for air reconnaissance over our Eastern coast from Cuban bases. And we see the Soviets and Cuba building a war machine in Nicaragua that dwarfs the forces of all their neighbors combined. Let's not fool ourselves: This war machine isn't being built to make Central America safe for democracy. It isn't being built to pursue peace, economic, or social reform. It's being built, by their own boasts, to impose a revolution without frontiers.

This is not *my* problem, it is *our* problem. But if we pull together, we can solve it. As I announced yesterday, I'm appointing a bipartisan commission on Central America. And let us resolve today: There must be no more captive nations in this hemisphere.

With faith as our guide, we can muster the wisdom and will to protect the deepest treasures of the human spirit: the freedom to build a better life in our time, and the promise of life everlasting in His kingdom. Aleksandr Solzhenitsyn told us, "Our entire earthly existence is but a transitional stage in the movement toward something higher, and we must not stumble and fall, nor must we linger, on one rung of the ladder."

With your help, we will stand shoulder to shoulder, and we'll keep our sights on the farthest stars.

Thank you very much and God bless you all.

Notes

Chapter 1

1. Luke 21:24b.
2. James 5:7–8, KJV paraphrased.

Chapter 2

1. *Reagan,* Lou Cannon, G. P. Putnam's Sons, New York, p. 188.
2. Ibid., p. 240.
3. *The Real Reagan,* Frank van der Linden, William Morrow & Co., Inc., New York, p. 27.
4. *The Reagans,* Peter Hannaford, Coward-McCann, Inc., New York, p. 302.
5. "White House Invokes 'damage-control' policy to protect Reagan," David Broder, *Washington Post,* 15 November 1981.
6. *Reagan,* p. 348.
7. *The Secret Kingdom,* Pat Robertson, Thomas Nelson, Nashville, p. 138.
8. Drew Parkhill, CBN economics specialist, 1 June 1983.
9. *U.S. News & World Report,* May 23, 1983, p. 21.
10. Ibid., p. 20.

Chapter 3

1. *Sincerely, Ronald Reagan,* edited by Helene von Damm, Berkley Books, New York, p. 88.
2. Ibid., p. 26.
3. Ibid., p. 93.
4. *The Real Reagan,* p. 26.
5. 1 Cor. 2:14.
6. *The Real Reagan,* p. 26.
7. 2 Cor. 6:1.
8. *The Real Reagan,* p. 35.
9. Phil. 2:12.
10. Eph. 2:10.

11. Psalm 139:13–16.
12. Phil. 2:13.
13. 1 Cor. 12:1.
14. Rom. 12:1–2.
15. *Sincerely, Ronald Reagan,* p. 88.

Chapter 4

1. *The Real Reagan,* p. 66.
2. Ibid., p. 67.
3. Heb. 10:24b–25.
4. *The Real Reagan,* p. 66.
5. Ibid., p. 72.
6. Psalm 106:2–5, KJV.
7. *The Real Reagan,* p. 26.
8. John 1:12–13.
9. "God, Home, and Country," Herbert E. Ellingwood, *Christian Life,* November, 1980, p. 24.
10. Ibid.

Chapter 5

1. *Long Time Gone,* Curt Smith, Icarus Press, South Bend, 1982, p. 80.
2. Matt. 25:14–28.
3. Matt. 25:29.
4. *The Secret Kingdom,* Pat Robertson, Thomas Nelson Publishers, Nashville, 1982, p. 123–24.
5. *Reagan,* p. 93–94.
6. *The Real Reagan,* p. 78.
7. *Christian Life,* November 1980, p. 52–54.
8. *Reagan,* p. 182–83.
9. *When the Going Was Good!* Jeffrey Hart, Crown Publishers Inc., New York, p. 158 ff.
10. *The Real Reagan,* p. 150 ff.
11. *U.S. News & World Report,* May 5, 1980, p. 30.

Chapter 6

1. *Decision,* Billy Graham, April, 1983, p. 1–2.
2. Ezek. 16:49–50.
3. *The Secret Kingdom,* p. 21–22.
4. *The Wealth of Families,* George Gilder, edited by Carl A. Anderson and William J. Gribbin, American Family Institute, Washington.
5. Prov. 22:4.
6. Matt. 5:5.
7. John 10:10.
8. Isa. 58:6–8.
9. *False Presence of the Kingdom,* Jacques Ellul, The Seabury Press, New York, 1972.
10. Matt. 5:14.

11. Luke 22:24–27.
12. Rom. 13:1.
13. 2 Chron. 7:14.
14. Letter to the French Ministry, Benjamin Franklin, March, 1778.

Chapter 7

1. 1 Cor. 2:14.
2. *Reagan,* p. 404–5.
3. John 4:34.
4. Matt. 6:10.
5. Josh. 1:6–9.
6. *Living the Lord's Prayer,* Everett L. Fullam, Chosen Books, Lincoln, Va. p. 84.
7. Psalm 106:15, KJV.
8. Col. 2:10.
9. *Living the Lord's Prayer,* p. 77.
10. Ibid., p. 81–82.

Chapter 8

1. TV Interview with George Otis of High Adventure Ministries, Van Nuys, Calif.
2. Lev. 19:18, KJV, cf. Luke 10:25–37.
3. Eph. 2:8.
4. Isa. 40:29, 31, KJV.
5. "The Right Reverend Ronald Reagan," Hugh Sidey, *Time,* March 21, 1983, p. 18.
6. Francis X. Clines, *New York Times,* Feb. 10, 1983.

Chapter 9

1. Matt. 16:18, KJV.
2. Matt. 4:19–20.
3. Luke 9:23.
4. Luke 9:26.
5. Matt. 5:13.

Chapter 11

1. 1 Thess. 5:2.
2. 1 Thess. 5:9–10.
3. 1 Thess. 5:11.

Chapter 12

1. "Why Conservatives Govern in Name Only," by P. T. Bauer, *The Wall Street Journal,* editorial page, March 29, 1983.
2. *Back to Basics,* Burton Yale Pines, William Morrow & Co. Inc., New York, 1982, p. 321.
3. Ibid., p. 321.

4. "Politics and the New Class," by Jeane J. Kirkpatrick, *Society, p. 43, January, 1979.*
5. *Back to Basics,* p. 320.
6. Ibid., p. 324–25.
7. Ibid., p. 325.
8. "The Mass Media," by James Hitchcock, *The Human Life Review,* Spring, 1983, p. 41–42, excerpted from *What Is Secular Humanism?* Servant Books, Ann Arbor, Michigan, 1982.
9. *Back to Basics,* p. 323–34.
10. Mark 13:5.
11. Matt. 24:4–5.
12. 1 Cor. 3:11.
13. *A Christian Manifesto,* Francis A. Schaeffer, Crossway Books, Westchester, Illinois, 1981, 1. 17–18.
14. Ibid., p. 24.

Chapter 13

1. "God, Home, and Country," Herbert E. Ellingwood, *Christian Life,* November, 1980, p. 50.
2. *Sincerely, Ronald Reagan,* p. 91.
3. *Reagan in Pursuit of the Presidency,* Doug and Bill Wead, Haven Books, Plainfield, N.J., 1980, p. 174.
4. Ibid., p. 170.
5. Reagan's speech to the N.A.E.
6. *Time,* March 21, 1983, p. 18.
7. 1 Cor. 2:14.
8. Col. 1:17.
9. CBN "700 Club" interview, 8 September 1983.
10. Deut. 4:29.
11. *A Christian Manifesto,* p. 132–33.
12. Isa. 58:9b–12.
13. Isa. 58:13–14.
14. Joel 2:15–17.
15. Joel 2:18–20.
16. Joel 2:23–29.
17. Joel 2:30 ff.
18. Matt. 16:3.
19. *World MAP Digest,* November-December, 1982, Burbank, California, p. 2 ff.
20. *A Christian Manifesto,* p. 33.

Chapter 14

1. 1 Timothy 2:1–2.
2. Gallup Survey for CBN, Gallup Organization Inc., Princeton, N.J., September, 1983.
3. *God's Politician,* Garth Lean, Darton, Longman & Todd, London 1980, p. 72.
4. Gallup Survey for CBN.
5. God's Politician, p. 72–73.

Bob Slosser was born in Frederick, Oklahoma, in 1929. After taking a degree in journalism at the University of Maine, he became a sports reporter with *The Evening Commercial* in Bangor, Maine, soon becoming the sports editor. Working his way up through small northeastern papers, he landed in New York City in 1955. Starting as a copy editor for *The New York World-Telegram and Sun,* he eventually became the night news editor, and in 1959 moved uptown to *The New York Times.* Although he worked periodically in most of the major news areas, he concentrated on national news during his twelve years with *The Times.* He was assistant national editor before being transferred to *The Times'* Washington Bureau during the height of the Watergate investigations.

He left *The Times* in 1975 to become founding editor of *The National Courier,* a significant but short-lived experiment in Christian journalism. Although he had been a co-author of *The Road to the White House* in 1965 (an account of the Goldwater-Johnson confrontation), his first book with a Christian perspective was undertaken during *The National Courier* days. It was *The Miracle of Jimmy Carter,* a best-selling collaboration with White House correspondent Howard Norton, exploring the rise of the little-known Georgia politician to national leadership. Nine books followed in short order, ranging across the full spectrum of Christian activity, including *Child of Satan, Child of God, Miracle in Darien,* and *The Secret Kingdom* (with Pat Robertson), and now *Reagan Inside Out.*

He lives with his wife, Gloria, to whom he has been married since 1950, in a rambling house on Linkhorn Bay in Virginia Beach, Virginia. They have four grown children and four grandchildren. As well as Christian perspectives on world events and issues, Slosser's interests include literature, music, and sports. He plays a scrambling, inconsistent game of tennis.